INTO WHOLENESS

The Path of Deep Imagery

Eligio Stephen Gallegos, PhD

Moon Bear Press

VELARDE, NM USA

Into Wholeness: The Path of Deep Imagery
Eligio Stephen Gallegos, PhD

Printing History
1st printing Winter 2001
2nd printing Spring 2018

Moon Bear Press
Box 468
Velarde, NM 87582

Into Wholeness/ E.S. Gallegos. -- 2nd ed.
ISBN-10: 0-944164-49-8
ISBN-13: 978-0-944164-49-5

For Mary

Contents

APOLOGIA

My friend, Mel Bucholtz, said of my book, *Animals of the Four Windows*, that he experienced it upon the first reading as if it had been extruded under great pressure. I understood him exactly. Perhaps not in the way he intended but in my own way. For I do feel a tremendous pressure to put forth my thoughts in order that other people may have a glimpse of the terrain that finds its way into my experience. The pressure is one of having found the terrain so valuable for myself that I wish to share it at once with someone else, not unlike spying an oasis after trudging through desert for most of my life: Hey! There's water over here. There really is! Come drink! Come drink!

I am usually at a tremendous loss, because the urgency strikes me so intensely. I wish to brook no delay, yet there is the need to churn out the words on my computer where I am sure that each thing I say could have been said much more clearly, or more thoroughly, or could have been better researched and detailed from an academic standpoint, or that I should take the time to follow the implications which arise with every idea. And yet there is the urgency of time: These things need to be known right now!

Then there is the way my own mind works. Because in the truest sense I don't think these things up, they come to me unbidden and make their way either suddenly or stealthily into my awareness, frequently at times that are the most unsuitable for writing: while soaking in the hot tub under the night sky at River Spirit, while reading something totally disconnected, while talking to someone, while driving along the New Mexico highway. The thoughts come rushingly or fleetingly or wispily, and I must then tease them forth again when I have paper or computer in front of me. And sometimes they just pour out while I am at the computer and take me to places I have not yet been, so that I am never quite certain where I am going and yet I feel an extreme urgency in putting forth the path that unfolds before my mental eye. I am not unlike being a passenger in a carriage pulled by a team of horses: while I think I know where we should go there is such an energy in the horses themselves that I could go nowhere without them and they seem to know the path better than I. Yet there are times that I sit at the computer and they do not budge: I don't know whether I am trying to take them in the wrong direction or if there is really no place to go at such moments.

I feel I may be discovering something that most writers must already know: that the craft is not my own but I belong to it; without it I can speak only clumsily. But when it wishes to offer itself I can only make myself available in deep thankfulness.

INTO WHOLENESS

When I wrote *Animals of the Four Windows* I originally subtitled it Integrating Thinking, Sensing, Feeling and Imagery into Wholeness, but as the time to print the book loomed closer and closer I realized that I could not include "into wholeness" in the subtitle because I myself was not yet whole, and what I strive to write is principally thoughts that come out of my own experience, having had a lifetime of education in which I listened to teachers teach other's thoughts but very few taught from their own experience. Since the writing of *Animals of the Four Windows* I have gone through numerous experiences, each of which left me a bit more whole than I had been before. Now I have come to a point in my life where I feel I can write from a place of moving more and more into wholeness, and so it is time to include those final two words that were omitted. Thus the title of this book, *Into Wholeness.*

INTRODUCTION

A spiritual path should necessitate a unique journey for each of us into the depths of our own soul. Sadly, often, pursuit of a spiritual path has come to entail more of an obedience to an external organization and an imitation of the stance of others rather than a truly individual exploration of soul. The discovery and uncovering of one's soul is an event that the modern Western world is just now beginning to return to. The hunger is there, has always been there, for coming home to the soul is also a coming into one's own wholeness. And in our modern world, where the most common description of what it is to be human, or even to be alive, mimics a mechanical device, the understanding of wholeness is sadly deficient and the paths there sadly lacking, however powerful the hunger may be.

The powerful need to belong to oneself and to belong in the universe are ultimately the same thing: the drive toward wholeness. And since this drive entails a pursuit toward fulfillment of the need to belong sometimes the need to belong is put first and people will join strange societies or cults in order to fulfill this need. However, belonging to a group maybe the opposite of pursuing one's wholeness, especially when the requirements of the group are those of obedience and imitation, as is the case with most cults and many organized religions.

The availability of a path toward wholeness which is uniquely tailored to the individual has long been lacking, and the thought of it may even sound paradoxical. How could one pursue a path that is uniquely personal, uniquely individual? Where would the feedback come from? How would a person know when they are on such a path and when they are off of it? What would the guidelines be? How would one come to arrive at such a path in the first place?

Surprisingly, the path has always been there in each of us. The feedback system is in place. Frequently the call into wholeness is very powerful. The invitation is simultaneously profound and mysterious, and it exists at the very heart of who we are. Why would it be that everything that grows, each animal, every flower, every tree, is invited and nurtured to grow into its wholeness, into its completeness, but not the human being?

Unfortunately, each of us has been trained to ignore the path, to fear the call, and to doubt the feedback. The system of training is called school. It requires conformity, obedience, a giving up of one's will to the teacher, a stepping away from one's true calling, and a learning to ignore the naturalness of the flow of one's own awareness. It requires an avoidance of one's own interests and a pursuit of commonality—on schedule, of course. Thus, the natural rhythm, the natural sense of timing, the organic beat that is in each of us is subordinated to the tick of the clock.

However, the path to wholeness is not subjected to that tick. It is a path of discovery, of ongoing recovery and of a natural uncovering, unfolding, and blossoming. The source of the path is in the very seed-kernel of who we are, has been with us from the beginning, and continues to summon and beckon throughout our lives. It requires from us relationship, true relationship, not the contrived obedience and conformity that were instilled in us in the name of child rearing. This true relationship requires being who and where we are and communicating that directly. For relationship is at the heart of coming into wholeness. We cannot get there by ownership, but only by relationship, a deep relationship with our own individual experiences.

Working within the layers of the Deep Imagination is the most powerful path to emotional healing, growing into maturity, and coming into balance with one's true being that I am familiar with. It is the path which leads us into our own wholeness. It is the avenue to our aliveness.

WHY DEEP IMAGERY?

There are many approaches available to seekers of wholeness today. There are those that rely on modifying our patterns of thinking and offer methods that are language based. Some occupy thinking by encouraging one to repeat phrases; others suggest going to the polarity of a negative thought and attempting to eliminate it through creating its opposite polarity. For example, replacing "I am a failure" with "I am a success." Others involve the development of behavioral or ceremonial patterns that are oriented around the body instead of around thinking, e.g. Yoga positions. The approach of deep imagery is different from these in that it involves the development of a relationship with a deep dimension of knowing, that of the spontaneous occurrence of deep imagery. Deep imagery entails a wisdom that is deeper and more universal than conceptual thought or language. The wisdom of deep imagery emanates from aliveness itself.

Working with the deep imagination involves respecting the uniqueness of each person's imagery and the development of a relationship between one's thinking and the natural spontaneous freedom of the deep imagination. The deep imagination, when allowed to participate in our knowing equally with the other ways of knowing (thinking, sensing, and feeling) can unify all of our ways of knowing around a singular reality, including the inner. This pathway, which I understand as that of aliveness itself, has brought us through the evolution of uncountable varieties of living forms to our presence today on this earth as humans. The pathway therefore brings with it the knowing and wisdom of every form of aliveness that has formed the passageway.

Wholeness from this perspective entails a universal respect for aliveness as an experiential dimension that is always in flow, always changing, always evolving and developing. Aliveness cannot be static. Yet, often, a spiritual path is portrayed as a predictable event or map. We thus overlook the fact that the path is unique to every person who walks it. The uniqueness of each individual's path to wholeness has frequently been sacrificed on the altar of commonality. Yet, we cannot arrive at our wholeness by imitating each other but only by making that singular journey to the very center of our living being and recognizing and respecting our differences and creative uniqueness.

In my own work animals frequently appear spontaneously in the deep imagination. Yet deep imagery is not confined to my own experience. Other people I work with have met religious and historical figures, as well as natural events and objects, geometric shapes and colors. In the deep imagination, they are all alive and embedded with a knowing and wisdom appropriate to the individual journey. These encounters in the deep imagination show us the depth and beauty and knowingness of aliveness itself. Frequently an alignment ensues involving the melting of the rigidity of the conceptual map that we carry around and a deepening of the wisdom of aliveness itself as the grand integrator. A realignment deep within the individual brings him or her back to a greater recognition of the utter uniqueness of aliveness on this earth and in the Universe. The recognition that aliveness dominates this earth leads to an understanding that aliveness is one of the fundamental properties of the Universe. We are a dimension of it, each one of us, uniquely so.

The peak of that mountain formed of the wisdom of aliveness must be arrived at individually. Then we can see that the path differs for everyone. All trees grow toward the sun but each in its unique way.

By developing an open and direct relationship with our deep imagination, we open ourselves to that wisdom that dwells in aliveness itself. The deep imagination carries within itself the potential of all experience. Not just the experience of this short lifetime that we take to be our own, individually, but the experience of that entire path that aliveness has traversed from the very beginning, from the origin of life itself.

Thirty years ago I was given a great gift, a gift that began the reorganization of my life, of my being, of my presence in the world, of my thinking. The gift I received was that of working with the deep imagination through my chakra power animals. The chakra animals arrived spontaneously and began the long path of healing to return me to the core of who I have always been. The experience of meeting the Chakra animals changed me and gave my life an entirely new direction. It initiated a return, a rebalancing, a realignment of who I am. I meet with these animals regularly in my deep imagination and they supported me upon a healing path that was not only profound but also astounding.

Since publication of the first edition of Into Wholeness my inner life has continued to grow and develop, especially regarding the primary theme of this work, injuries and their healing into wholeness. I am convinced that every injury involves a separation. The prototype would be a broken bone. If you break a bone it involves a breach between two (at least) segments of what had previously been a single bone. The two pieces need to be held in their original position until a new bond is formed, until the two pieces have knit together into a single structure once again.

A similar bonding is necessary in the case of an emotional injury. In an emotional injury something is separated within the person which needs to once again be joined. The search for a method of rejoining would entail a retelling of the history of psychotherapy. Unfortunately, save for a few fine people, one dimension has been all but ignored in this search, the underlying membrane of the deep imagination. It is through the deep imagination that we gain access to the fabric of our own being and the capacity to support those structures in the positions necessary for their rejoining into wholeness.

The human being is an animal like any other save for the fact of our ability to abstract, to objectify, to pose possibilities, to render the world into a series of sounds and marks that then become a substitute for the world itself. Unlike the other animals, we have to a great extent removed ourselves from the immediacy of our experience, which is always the point of contact with the present moment. We have strung ourselves out in time and space through our ability to think, not recognizing that we must always return to the place of our anchorage in the present moment, the immediacy of our present experience.

Thus thinking also becomes a breach between our being and our connection to the rest of creation. It is not that thinking must be removed in order for this breach to be healed, but that thinking needs to return voluntarily to its balanced position within the wholeness of who we are.

The changes in this second edition are primarily the addition of a few chapters at the end of this book which complete an early theme in my life, my experiences with my father and my puzzlement and eventual rage and terror concerning the ways I was treated. I am grateful that this path has led me to the ultimate understanding of those forces in his life that impinged upon my own.

I thank the Great Spirit of the Universe for the path I have been given, every step of the way. In the following chapters I present glimpses of these experiences, conveyed as best I can in words and language, in order to indicate the existence of a path to wholeness through deep imagery. I could have presented the stories of other people as well, for many people have blossomed from following this path, but I am most intimately aware of my own and I respect the rights of others to indicate their own paths. In fact, I encourage them to do so.

CHAPTER ONE

THE PATH OF DEEP IMAGERY

The hopelessness that I felt for much of my life, the terror, the total non-comprehension of what was happening with me or to me, the vast loneliness, and the thought that other people knew what was going on but I did not, are a few of the things that prompt me to write this book. I put myself forth as the guinea pig, not with a sense of anything congratulatory, but for the sake of others who have experienced similar things in their lives to know that there is hope. For me to have come to the place in myself where I now live was at one time incomprehensible to me, impossible even to imagine, unbelievable. For I have come to a place within myself, to a place of relationship with all of my various dimensions and characteristics, to a place of solitude within myself and appreciation for the people around me, to a place of intimate relationship with all things and with the Universe itself, and for the first time since I was born I am at home.

This is the path to wholeness, a building of relationship with all our various dimensions. It is a path open to everyone. Deep within each person is the knowing of the possibility of transformation, of arriving at a place where rather than continuing one's everyday walk in the world one must now go deep within where a gathering occurs, a gathering of all of one's dimensions which then merge into a single whole, a whole that is greater than the sum of the previous parts. This possibility of transformation is readily available to us, through the Path of Deep Imagery. It shows itself readily when we actively engage in a relationship with our imagery.

If we are willing to approach our imagery openly, without pre-judging it, with a willingness to learn from it rather than treating it like we already know what it is about, we may find that it is the lost jewel we have hoped might exist somewhere. If we can approach imagery with a sense of humility, with an openness and willingness to learn, we may discover something startling: we find that we encounter a profound teacher of the kind we had always wished for; A teacher who knows us intimately yet non-judgmentally, a teacher who knows that we learn in our own unique way, a teacher that knows how to structure situations so that we are engaged from deep within, so that we are enticed to learn, rather than feeling as if something were imposed on us, and a teacher who is concerned not only with our learning but also with our growing. We each carry such a teacher deep within who we are.

But teacher is perhaps a poor word to use for this deep inner dimension, for too often teachers have been our enemies, our antagonists, petty tyrants who do not seem to have our best interests at heart but only their survival within a system that is intent on perpetuating its own organization rather than really engaging the student and holding his or her growth and development as paramount. Perhaps a mature and knowing friend would be a better way of portraying that deep dimension, but even here we fail to convey the profound aliveness of this friend, the sense of spirited awareness, and the lovely warm humor that bubbles forth spontaneously from him (or her, or it). For this place of deep imagery has no restrictions. It can employ anything at all to help us in our growing. It is not bound by the constraints of space and time. This place is not fixed by a mathematical logic, it instead emanates from a deep organic logic, a living logic, the same logic unfolds the blossom and that holds the universe together, inclusive of all of life.

The only requirement for engaging such a teacher, friend, wise and living presence, is that we be willing to communicate our experience truthfully and to allow time and awareness for this presence to respond.

We all can go to our imagery voluntarily and say to it, "Hello. Are you willing to speak to me?" Our imagery may take the form of a long lost friend and say, "I've been waiting all this time for you to come back to me." And we find ourselves dissolving in tears for something beautiful in us that has been rejected for far too long.

Our deepest imagery is naturally alive. Why would it not be? We are living beings and imagery is a deep and ancient part of who we are. It works with us to help heal the emotional injuries that have been part of our lives, injuries that in many cases helped pull us away from our wholeness, from being in touch with who we are at all levels, injuries that involved giving ourselves to an external world as a way of avoiding further injury in the future. Imagery knows how to help us heal these injuries and return us to an honoring of the fullness of our natural awareness.

The path that has been forged within myself, and also by others, through our relationship with imagery, can never be fully documented. The few scattered memories that I describe here were not my life but only what was held in memory. The journeys I record are not the experiences themselves but only stories that can be shared in written words. And yet, the fabric that is woven in this book does have a pattern. It is in itself a potential map for others. It is with this focus that I tell this story.

My journey into wholeness has come about by following a singular path, a path of honoring and engaging directly with the deep dimension of imagination that exists in me. This path also exists within every individual. The route is unique for each person, since it is based on one's own unique experiences, but the direction is true and unerring: through the healing of emotional injuries, the gathering of lost or hidden elements, and ultimately their integration into a single whole.

CHAPTER 2

MANY ALIVENESSES

The idea that we need to gather ourselves, our being, into a single whole may sound strange to you. When we think of ourselves as being alive, we most often conceive of it as singular experience. We already believe we are a single whole. To understand how the deep imagination works, we need to begin by becoming aware that humans contain many alivenesses. We need to be aware that thinking, as process, tends towards a simplistic understanding. Aliveness is much more complex than the place towards which our thinking flows. After all, thinking has emanated out of aliveness, not aliveness out of thinking. If we allow our thinking to take into account the true uniqueness and flexibility of our aliveness we can begin recognizing that, as Walt Whitman observed, "I contain multitudes."

One difficulty in recognizing our multiple alivenesses is that they usually flow relatively smoothly together. Thinking tends to overlook their differences and understands them as seamless, so that we think of our aliveness as unitary rather than as complex. We rarely have reason to notice that our aliveness is in fact, multiple. Indeed, it isn't usually until our alivenesses are in conflict with one another that we are alerted to their great variety. Such conflicts demonstrate a need for healing and growing, a need to allow inner dialogue, a need, that in my experience can most easily be met through engaging with deep imagery. However, we typically try to resolve such conflicts through our thinking, and attempt to impose a single understanding whereas we rightfully should enter the subjective realm and encounter the alivenesses themselves directly.

The Hindus have a complex view of how aliveness works. They recognize that there is a system of alivenesses that can be contacted through various body locations. They term these alivenesses 'wheels of energy' (Chakras), but we can also think of them as alivenesses. My own exploration in this realm has brought me to recognize that these alivenesses are readily recognized when we approach them through the knowing of the deep imagination, that is, the realm of imagination that is deeper than fantasy or free association. This realm is free and relatively independent, not under our voluntary control. This 'deep imagination' is responsive and willing to communicate with our thinking. However it is deeper than thinking and functions at the level of imagery rather than concepts and ideas. When thinking and the deep imagination function in harmony we find ourselves plunged into a much deeper, wiser, and more mature perspective.

The difficulty that we have in initially understanding these different layers is due to the fact that we have been thoroughly trained to bring everything into thought. Our thinking has become overly automatic. During this process thinking has itself developed numerous protective and defensive tactics. Freud called these 'ego defense mechanisms.' It would be better if we thought of them as childhood survival tactics, developed for our survival among larger adults whether parents, teachers, or dictators, who have a propensity to control.

This current book, 'Into Wholeness,' presents a series of examples, mostly taken from my own experience, in healing the automatic emotional reactions, avoidances, and misperceptions, that emanate from being raised in a culture that overly used punishment as a means of training obedience. Additionally, it is a culture that developed an over reliance on thinking as an adequate interface with living nature, including human nature.

Our healing, our growing, our maturing requires that we deepen our understanding of what it is to live a life that streams with the various currents of our alivenesses. In doing so, language and thinking loosen their hold on us and we develop a more unified experience of support and harmony that emanates from within. Then our very being, our existence, comes home to knowing its own wisdom, and we recognize that aliveness comes with its own direction. We then realize that we cannot form a healthy social union unless we have also grown into a being whose inner community of alivenesses are mature, balanced, and whole. Once we are in harmony within ourselves, individually, only then can we hope to arrive at that social communion that naturally reflects our inner being. We must first be at home in ourselves before we can be fully at home with other beings.

CHAPTER 3

ROOTS

The tale I heard tell was that Stephen Powers had been asked by his father, Col. Joshua Dever Powers, to leave Kentucky and go out to the New Mexico Territory to take over supervision of a gold mine in which Joshua Dever held half interest. Stephen had just graduated from the University of Tennessee and did not want to go that long way from his home in Kentucky, but his father's wishes were more than a request. Travel at that time, into the land that had recently been acquired from Mexico as a territory, was by wagon train. Not knowing what to do and fretting over the long journey, Stephen, walking along a lonely road, was offered a ride in a horse drawn carriage by a friend of the family, Neville Pendleton, a woman a few years older than he. Pouring his heart out, Stephen confessed to her that he had already asked his girlfriend if she would marry him and make the journey and had just been refused. "That's no problem," Neville answered, "I'll marry you and we can make the journey together!" Whether Stephen accepted her offer with thanks and appreciation or as the only possible option will perhaps never be known. However it stands, this was how my maternal grandparents began the trek from Kentucky out to what would later become the state of New Mexico. At least that was the story I heard told.

The gold mine, located in Lincoln County, New Mexico, apparently never produced much gold, so Stephen, having a degree in civil engineering, moved to Las Vegas, New Mexico (not the gambling city in the state of Nevada) where he eventually became superintendent of the water works. There he and Neville raised their family of seven children, where my mother, the next to last, was born in 1906.

Las Vegas was the last stop on the Santa Fe Trail before Santa Fe itself, the same Santa Fe trail that Stephen and Neville had followed on their journey out west. And it was a thriving city, at that time being larger than Albuquerque: thriving, that is, until the great depression.

My mother, Katherine Juliet Powers, was an avid student, loved to read and learn and was a published poet. In the little village where I grew up she was always called by her nickname, Coy. She came to the village of Los Lunas at the age of eighteen, to help her older sister, Ruth, at the birth of Ruth's first child. My aunt Ruth had married Joseph Tondre, a federal marshal whose own parents had left France to establish a trading post in the small Indian pueblo of Isleta, about seven miles north of where I was born. I remember Aunt Ruth as a patient and lovely woman, and her two youngest daughters, Ruthie and Katy, were great friends with whom I used to love to play kick the can.

Los Lunas is the only town in the United States to have a southern mansion built out of adobes, pillars and all. The town was named for Solomon Luna rather than for the moon. Solomon was a wealthy sheep farmer whose family home just happened to stand exactly where the Santa Fe Railway wished to lay its tracks on the way to California. His wife refused to allow a railroad to run through her house until the railway made her an offer she couldn't refuse. She was offered a tour through the United States, on their trains, of course, and on her trip she could choose any house she liked and the railroad company would build her the exact duplicate to replace her own, although in a different location. That is how she acquired a southern mansion. The Mansion is now a restaurant.

My uncle Fred said that the first time my mother saw my father, Eligio, he was riding a white horse and she thought he was the most handsome man she had ever seen. Her early poetry emanates an intensity of passion that surprised me when I first read it, but of course I didn't know her in those early days. My father originally spelled his name (and mine) Elijio, a derivative of Elijah which means "he who was elected." He was indeed a handsome man. My sister, Rosalie, wrote after his funeral, that he looked like he had been carved out of ancient ivory lying in his coffin.

Eligio was the eldest in a family of thirteen children. His father, Jesus Gallegos, was sheriff of Valencia County, and a large man who wore a size forty-four gun belt. Jesus' family was of Native American origin, although for historic reasons, they claimed to have come from Spain in the early 1800's and thus lived as part of the Hispanic community[1]. My grandmother, Martina Marquez Gallegos, was the daughter of an Amerindian father who was known to me as Papa Juan, and who occasionally served as a scout for the wagon trains between Santa Fe and St. Louis, being gone on that run for six months at a time.

---

1 In the first edition of this book, I wrote that Jesus' family came from Spain. Our family story had asserted that Loret(t)o Gallegos had come from there in the early 1800's. Since then, through DNA analysis and a deeper search into the local church and census records, we now know this to be untrue. My paternal family line is Native American, although de-tribalized. Given where I grew up in the Los Lunas/Los Lentes area of New Mexico, my family is most likely of *Genízaro* descent, as such peoples were known as under Spanish rule. Likewise, Tomé, from where my grandmother Martina came, was also a *Genízaro* village. In many ways this information was both deeply surprizing and also made total sense to me. I will perhaps write more about it at another time. I thank my niece, Kathy D'Assis for her diligent search through local records to trace our family line and my wife, Mary Diggin Ph.D, for her research into the history of NM and particularly the *Genízaros* which was partly to inspire her doctoral dissertation and also her forthcoming book .

Her mother I only knew as Mamalita. Mamalita was a mysterious woman who had names for all of her animals, even the chickens, and used to talk to them. It was said that they responded to her. Both Papa Juan and Mamalita were deeply kind people.

Papa Juan died when I was three years old. His wake, held in the little adobe house where he had lived, haunted me for many years. The largest room had been emptied of furniture except for the chairs borrowed from the neighbors which lined the walls. People were sitting in them talking in hushed voices. It was evening and his coffin stood on two low stools in the very center of the room. The house had no electricity and the room was dimly lit with candles and a kerosene lamp.

I was very curious about the coffin. I knew that Papa Juan was dead although I didn't quite know what that was and I knew also that his body was in the coffin. Although the coffin was open it was about as high as me. I told my mother that I wanted to go look inside and she said for me to go ahead. I left where she was sitting and walked slowly toward the coffin, feeling a dread rise in me the closer I got. Suddenly, just as I reached it, I whirled away and ran back to my mother's side. I would not approach it again although I was now more curious than ever.

My birth certificate, written in my mother's hand, indicates that I was named Elijio Gallegos, Jr., at birth. At some point Stephen was interjected as a middle name, after her father, and the Jr. was dropped. I don't know when this change occurred, nor whether there was any controversy around it, since from my earliest days I remember having been called Stephen.

I was the second of their four children. My oldest sister, Juliet Pendleton, was four years older than me and died of Leukemia when she was fifty-four. Rosalie Loretta, four years younger than I was, and Neville Ruth, four years younger than Rosalie, show that my mother was adept both at birth control and at the spacing of children. Rosalie currently lives in Tucson, Arizona, and Ruthie, sadly, died last year (2017). She had been the first woman to ever run for mayor of Los Lunas, losing by only 100 votes.

The home in which I spent most of my childhood had been built by my father on land that was given to him as a wedding present by Uncle Joe. It was a three room adobe house with a bedroom, kitchen and living room and was located about a mile from the village of Los Lunas. Strictly speaking it was right at the edge of the neighboring farming village of Los Lentes.

The kitchen had a built in sink which was unusual in homes at that time and on the counter next to the sink was a hand pump that did not work during my lifetime. We had no electricity, however my father acquired a giant diesel engine which was to power the generator that would supply the current for a six-volt electrical system that was already wired into the house. I remember my father powering up the generator when it was first installed and we gloried in having electric lights for about a week. Before and after that our evenings were illuminated by kerosene lamps.

The living room was unique in that the front door stood in the center of a round wooden frame which had once been the inside of an oil well. Juliet and I slept in the living room. Two extra rooms, built over a period of many years, were eventually completed and became a bedroom and a new kitchen. The old kitchen was then converted into a hallway, a bathroom, and a small room that I acquired as a bedroom. Later, after I left home, it became a closet.

My early chores were to pump water, the pump was outside, and bring it into the house in a bucket, to chop wood and bring in an armload and to bring in a bucket of coal. Our bathroom was an outhouse that was more modern than most in that it boasted a hinged cover that could close over the seat when not in use. We installed an indoor bathroom for Juliet's wedding when she was eighteen. Not long before that we had acquired electric lights and natural gas.

As a child I can remember one afternoon, a brilliantly clear and sunny afternoon, standing outside of our house, listening to a bird standing on a fence post singing. Its song was as brilliant as the sun piercing through the clarity of that afternoon and left me stunned with the realization of the magnificence of existence. "How amazing," I thought to myself, "that anything at all exists!" It was obvious to me that there could just as easily be nothing, and so existence itself was a magnificent gift.

There were experiences I had as a young child for which there were absolutely no words. One was the sudden hush that would fall in the late afternoon. At that crease of day where evening first perceptibly falls the entire world would be absolutely still. Eternity showed itself to me and to anyone who was willing to step into it for that brief but everlasting moment. Returning stunned to the talk and general activity of the everyday world I was confused that no one spoke of this awesome event; in fact, there seemed to be a moment of embarrassment. It just had no place to fit into that world that we were busily creating through our activities.

I also spent much time fascinated by the dust swirling in the bright rays of sunshine that came through the windows in the afternoon. The dust had its own aliveness and moved endlessly here and about. And mirrors also intrigued me. I would peek around the edge of the mirror, astounded by the fact that things not directly before the mirror could find their way into it.

As night fell sheets were hung in the windows of our curtainless house, at least in the kitchen where we all gathered around the kerosene lamp, even though we were a mile from our nearest neighbor and we had a dog that would bark at anyone's approach. It was an Aladdin lamp with a glowing woven fabric around the flame which spread the light evenly so that it did not flicker and which I always found mysterious. Why didn't it burn up?

The dark seemed endless, broken only by the bark of a dog and the answer of another miles away creating a tangible fabric through that invisible void, letting each other know of their continuing existence and assumption of doggy duties.

One of my earliest memories is of lying in my crib in the room next to the kitchen, awakening and calling in the only way I knew how for someone to come get me and bring me into that human gathering around the lighted lamp. When no one came I cried out again. I know now they were hoping I would go back to sleep. Eventually my father came into the room. My elation quickly changed to confusion as he picked me out of my crib and spanked me and put me back down. This was the first of an ongoing series of never understood punishments. I know my mother never understood his continuous punishment of me although she had her Freudian theories.

My mother was warm and loving, especially when she was home alone with her children. One late snowy afternoon after my sisters and I had exhausted ourselves outside throwing snowballs and building a snowman we came inside to put on warm pajamas and eat delicious sugar cookies straight out of the oven.

My mother would read us a chapter a night just before we went to sleep out of books that she loved: The Jungle Books, Little Women, Little Men, Tom Sawyer and Huckleberry Finn. Warm and glowing, we would fall asleep.

CHAPTER 4

EARLY INJURY

I was four and my sister, Juliet, was eight. It was late summer. Juliet and I had gone with my father to the field, an acre of fertile land a quarter of a mile from our house, to irrigate. The acre was planted half in alfalfa and half in melons, squash, corn, chile, and tomatoes which sustained us through the summer months. It was a fine evening, fresh and clear, with the clarity and depth that only New Mexico evenings can have.

Juliet and I were present and playful, and now that I think of it, we had probably come along at my mother's suggestion, so she could have some time to herself. She was pregnant at the time. My father, Eligio, was a man who had always planted and grown food from the earth.

The sun had just set, lingeringly, and as nighttime loomed my father told me and Juliet to go home as it was getting dark. We began the walk along the shoulder of highway 85 toward our house. I don't remember the walk at all, but we must have been spunky and playful. As we neared the house a car approached us from far ahead, headlights burning. As it came nearer I suddenly left Juliet's side, dashed into the center of the highway and stood there holding my arms out wide as if to stop it. The car braked abruptly to a halt in order to keep from hitting me and I ran back to Juliet's side feeling confident and cocky...but not for long. My father's yells and footsteps as he ran toward us let me know that I had done something wrong and Juliet and I took off running as fast as we could toward the house. As I ran I could hear the driver and my father exchange a few hurried words. I ran so fast that I lost the moccasins I was wearing.

By the time we arrived at the back door of our little adobe house (the front door was seldom used by us) my mother, in the fullness of her pregnancy, had emerged. My father arrived enraged and frightened, demanding to know why I had run out in front of that car. Of course, I myself didn't know why I had done it. It was just an impulsive action. Upon considered reflection I remember my earlier surprise when I first saw a traffic policeman in the middle of Central Avenue in Albuquerque. Cars didn't hit him but instead obeyed his directions. When he held his arms out to the sides the cars stopped. And I can remember having been asked by my uncles if I was going to grow up to be a sheriff like my grandfather Jesus. So the act may have been an expression of my unknowing curiosity about the viability of such a future, or it could have been done in order to impress my older sister with my daring and bravado.

My father didn't really want answers although both Juliet and I were thoroughly, although hurriedly, interrogated with many why's. "Why did you do that? Why didn't you keep him by your side? Why didn't you hold his hand? Didn't you know you could be killed?" And my mother, in all the turmoil, just wanted to know what had happened.

My father cut a switch, turned me over his knee and began to beat me. I was shocked by the intensity of the pain and I truly thought he intended to beat me to death. I don't know how long he beat me but I was frantic; I had never known such hurt. When he finally stopped beating me he took Juliet over his knee and beat her. Finally my father and mother went into the house.

Juliet was lying on a wooden bench outside under the apple tree sobbing. She was lying on her stomach because her backside hurt so much. I went over to comfort her, and to gain some comfort myself, two children, wrongfully punished, seeking solace. But she lashed out at me. "If you hadn't run out in front of that car I wouldn't have gotten whipped!"

I was alone. Friendless. Hurting more than I had ever hurt before. My mother put us to bed. I can remember her coming to me later to ask me where exactly I had lost my moccasins. She went looking for them with a flashlight but they were never found. I lay in that bed hurt and angry, and in my anger I swore that I would kill my father, I swore to God that I would kill my father if it was the last thing I ever did. I was seething, enraged, completely vengeful. I would take a knife and plunge it into him until he was dead. I would do that! As I lay there imagining my revenge my pain gradually subsided but then I became suddenly aware of what I was swearing: I had sworn to God that I would kill my father! That was a mortal sin! It was a sin for which there was no forgiveness! Even if I never did the act, the intention itself was a sin! I was doomed to burn in hell for all of eternity! The terror of my thoughts was vast, unending, I had come to a place in myself from which there was no escape. I spent the rest of the night in dread and terror.

By morning my seething feelings had subsided and I was relatively calm when I got up. But as soon as my father saw me he told me with tremendous forcefulness that from now on whenever anyone told me to do something I was to do it without any backtalk and without questioning it. I was not to answer back, I was only to obey. I couldn't understand why he was so upset over something that was already over but the laws he was laying down were to perpetuity. I found myself bound by them like the walls of a prison.

CHAPTER 5

CONFUSION & SEARCH

My childhood was filled with buried rage, little or no communication, a painful loneliness, feelings of worthlessness, alternating feelings of deadness and tremendous creativity, and a powerful feeling of need.

What seemed to be closest to the surface in me was a deep feeling of terror and shame. I longed for close relationships yet I had none. I was both thrilled by the thought that someone would care for me, would care to know me, could guide me in my growing, and terrified at the thought of it. I always had at least one good male friend, a buddy, who was usually courageous and kind. And I always felt both smart and dumb at the same time. Socially I was completely inept.

School was a place that I dreaded and where I felt under constant threat. And home, especially around my father, was not much different. I was quiet and never knew what to say in situations with people. My greatest solace was in being alone out under the large cottonwood trees that lined the banks of the irrigation ditch some distance behind our house.

I did love to play: cops and robbers, hiding go seek (as we called it), kick the can, usually with my sisters, Rosalie and Juliet, and sometimes with my cousins, Ruthie and Katy Tondre. When I was ten years old Orlando Valenzuela and I became lifelong friends. We would go horseback riding on Sundays, out into the hills, riding bareback, he on his horse, Prince, and me on my horse, Flicka. We were tentatively seeking those adventures of knighthood which we knew at the time only inherently.

Orlando, or Lando as I used to call him, lived over a mile away, and sometimes he would come over to my house or I would go to his. His family lived right along the irrigation ditch where there was a wonderful swimming hole and some evenings we would go swimming along with his brothers and sisters and any other friends that were visiting. I had learned to swim alone in the same irrigation ditch where it ran along behind my house. It was these friendships and playing that provided a modicum of sanity in my life.

When I was seven years old I fell madly in love with Nathalie who had beautiful big brown eyes. I longed to ask her to be my girl friend but I was painfully shy. If I could only find a time and place where we were alone together I would ask her, for I could hardly speak when she was with others. Finally, on a snowy day, she and I walked the few blocks together from the school to her house, alone at last. But the only thing I could muster the courage to do was to throw a snowball at her.

When I was a teenager I discovered leatherwork and took to it immediately. I loved making things, belts, wallets, comb cases. I was good at leatherwork. I would usually make things and give them away to people as gifts but occasionally I would make something on order. One day two ladies arrived who had heard about my prowess and ordered a leather belt for someone named John as they had me carve his name on one of my belts. I became particularly adept at lacing the edges of leather pieces I had made with various patterns of braiding.

Later I discovered woodwork and wood carving and made a number of pieces of furniture, and in my early forties I began doing silver work. I have always loved crafts and the stance of the craftsman. I also drew quite well, and was a good cartoonist, sometimes drawing cartoons in school and selling them to school-mates. I felt guilty about accepting money for doing what I loved to do. I remember lying in bed at night, staring at the stuccoed adobe wall next to my bed, and seeing multitudes of faces in the roughness of the wall. My father looked upon comic books and cartoons as something foolish. My mother also said occasionally that artists did not earn much money.

School for me was torture. There was no place todo what I loved to do and what I was good at. And although I learned easily what I learned had nothing at all to do with what was happening in my life. I memorized individual facts that had nothing to do with one another, there was no underlying fabric holding it all together, and it was pure drudgery. And some of the teachers perpetuated their own ignorance as teaching. One of my teachers insisted that the pronunciation of "sword" was to pronounce "word"with an "s" before it! 'Swerred,' rather than 'sord,' as it should be pronounced! Teachers did have a difficult time with me for a while. Once I was made to stand out in the hall facing the wall. Another time I was stood up in front of the class and ridiculed by the teacher, something I curiously knew well as my father would not infrequently make me stand in front of him while he berated me, telling me how ashamed he was to have me for a son, how worthless I was, etc. I was not allowed to respond or answer or object, I was to stand in silence, but inwardly I was seething with a potent rage. Once he whipped me and then immediately said, "Now come here and tell me you love me." Although I did it I could feel something twist inside of me.

I survived school by going numb, becoming obedient, giving up any sense of my own direction, so that by the time I graduated from high school I had no idea what my interests were nor what I would do for a living. I went off to college which I found to be as dull and boring as high school. I drank and partied, failed several courses, put on a front of bravado, and after three semesters dropped out. Orlando got me a job as a laborer building houses where he worked. I had no idea that a laborers job was so long and difficult! After a few months of this backbreaking work Orlando and I joined the Air Force but we were sent to different posts.

Joining the Air Force was a saving grace. It removed me from my environment, provided the comradeship of good friends, and took me to Europe where I discovered a warmth and depth of ancient cultures, the beauty of music, and the magnificence of museums. I also began reading. During high school I had read only two books: The Bobbsey Twins in Vermont, which my Aunt Rose gave me, and The Three Musketeers, which one of my few good teachers, Mr. Farley, got me to read by making it a personal challenge. But in the Air Force, in Europe, I would visit the library and select books by feel, books about which I knew nothing at all, and began reading.

I came to Freud that way (whom I originally called Frood), and Dostoevsky, Will Durant, Voltaire, and history and philosophy. Most of my reading was selected by the feel of the book. I had no idea what I was getting into, but it was emotionally satisfying. I was seeking something, I didn't even know what, but there was a particular feeling when I was on the right track and would then read as much as I could by that particular author.

Shortly before being discharged from the Air Force, after spending three years in Europe, I encountered a textbook on psychology and felt excited about the topic. Here, finally, was an orientation that could shed some light on my state of mind.

When I returned to the United States in 1957, I was enthusiastic about learning, and understood finally that education and schools had originally been about learning, even though by the time of my early education they by then dealt primarily with order and obedience. On my way home to New Mexico I stopped to visit one of my Air Force buddies in Wisconsin, Lew Tusken. He was attending the University of Wisconsin. I sat in on some of his classes and knew that was where I wanted to go. I quickly applied for admission to UW, and after visiting my parents for a few weeks, moved to Wisconsin only to discover that my application had been denied because of several failing grades I had received when I was first in college.

I promptly requested a personal meeting with the registrar and was given an appointment with an assistant registrar. When we met I told her that I had matured considerably since getting those failing grades and that I was now enthusiastic about school and learning and also that I had taken a German Language course in which I had made an A. She told me that if I could produce a letter from the teacher in Germany from whom I had taken that course saying that I was a good student, that I could be admitted. I quickly went home and wrote such a letter to myself, took it to the assistant registrar, and she admitted me on double probation! I always loved that woman: a beautiful human being whose humanity was bigger than the rules of the University. She returned the letter to me when my probation was lifted.

The first trimester was difficult as I had to learn how to study and take exams while holding down a full time job as bartender. But I loved it! I would emerge from classes just thrilled. The University of Wisconsin had a policy at that time, I don't know if they still do, of requiring their full professors to teach lower division courses. So I took Introductory Psychology from Harry Harlow who had become renowned for his studies with baby monkeys and surrogate mothers. I also had a great interest in genetics, Joshua Lederberg was there at the time, and in mathematics and music and literature. My algebra professor suggested to me one day that I should consider mathematics as a major.

The psychology courses were full of interesting facts derived from experiments but somehow never involving the full human being. They were isolated facts. Something seemed to be lacking. I continued to take courses feeling that eventually I would understand about people (and particularly about myself). I toyed with the idea of taking a Master's degree in comparative literature which I loved. Here was a subject that did deal with people. The authors seemed to know more about people than the psychologists I was reading. But I know now that I possess a dogged persistence, and so I continued on in psychology, taking my BA at the University of Wisconsin, a Master's degree at New Mexico State University and a Ph.D. at Florida State University, where I majored in physiological psychology (the brain and sensory systems), with heavy emphasis on learning theory and experimental psychology. I was secretly interested in clinical psychology but stayed away from it because of a fear of my own craziness.

I must mention an interesting event that happened at Florida State. Part way through my studies I was to take an exam in order to qualify for the PhD track. The exam was both written and oral.

I passed the written portion with good marks. The oral portion was administered by a group of four or five professors. During the oral exam I froze up completely, became mute, knew the answers to the questions the professors were asking but could not utter a sound. I remember thinking that I should just leave, that I did not have the qualities for obtaining a PhD, but I just sat there frozen.

I came out of the exam so shaken by my behavior that I began to write a journal even though I was terrified of doing so. I didn't even know what I was going to write but I began by writing about my going mute during the exam and having no idea why. I was terrified that someone would find the journal and read it so I hid it well. I continued to write in the journal for years, not with any particular goal in mind other than understanding the intense emotional states I would find myself in. I would write primarily when I would find myself in an intense feeling that seemed to have no relation to what was going on in my life, which was frequent. I filled eight notebooks over those years. As an aside, the professors gave me a passing grade on my oral exam.

Upon my graduation I obtained a job as an associate professor in psychology at a small university in southern Georgia. It is astounding to me that I became a teacher, a professor, because I had a tremendous terror of standing before a class and teaching. I also felt I knew very little about psychology. On the outside I tried to appear confident and knowledgeable but on the inside I was filled with doubt and terror.

One positive event that happened during this time was visiting a friend I had met while we were both students at Florida State. He was a rare human being named Patrick de Sercey and he had become chairman of the Department of Philosophy at Valdosta State College. Pat, without intending to, introduced me to meditation. The meditation is one which was called "choice-less aware-ness" by Krishnamurti, or awareness without any object.

I was about to leave to return home when Pat said to me: "I was reading a book of essays last night and came upon one that reminded me exactly of you." At my request he retrieved the book but search as he would he could not find the essay that had re-minded him so much of me, so he loaned me the book. It was Jiddu Krishnamurti's Commentaries on Living (1960). I devoured the book, understanding perhaps a quarter of it. I did not find a single essay that particularly reminded me of myself. What I did experience was a deep appreciation for the awesome clarity and awareness of the author. I returned the book to Pat and asked him how Krishnamurti himself had become so clear and aware, as this was a state for which I greatly hungered.

"He sat on his ass for thirty years meditating!" Pat answered in his own inimitable style.

At my request Pat instructed me in meditation, which I began practicing immediately, and the following year we travelled to-gether to a Zen sesshin conducted by Philip Kapleau in Rochester, New York, where I received more official instruction in Zen med-itation. The beauty of the discipline to me at the time was that it provided me with a place I could go when I didn't understand what was going on. The powerful feelings would well up in me seeming to come out of nowhere and to have nothing to do with my everyday living, were thus provided a location in my life. On these occasions I would retreat as soon as I could to my medita-tion room and sit on my cushions facing the wall. Here I would allow myself to become as aware as possible, not trying to define or interpret what was happening in me but just letting myself experience it as fully as I could without judging the experience.

I discovered that if I did come to an understanding about what was happening in me, the understanding would usually follow the experience rather than precede it. I continued to meditate irregularly and do so to this day.

In academia, I advanced rapidly receiving tenure within two years and I was a full professor within six. I did not identify with the faculty, I felt many of them were quite petty, and I hated faculty meetings. I always sided with the students. I felt the students needed something that we were not providing. Somehow the intellectual stuff I was teaching, we were all teaching, was shallow and devoid of substance. I didn't know what to do but I had the profound feeling that I needed to leave the university.

I took a leave of absence after thirteen years of teaching to undertake a residency in psychotherapy at less than half of my usual salary. During my teaching career I had been able to follow my own interests and they tended more and more to veer in the direction of dreams, meditation, and imagery. So during my residency I began to work with imagery. There were only a few books on imagery available at the time. What was available seemed to me to be either overly erudite or piecemeal, lacking some kind of inherent organic underpinning. The best approaches to imagery I found at the time, were Jung's archetypal approach and Assagioli's Psychosynthesis. However, their theoretical approach, to my mind, was fundamentally social, and focused on imagery structures that could be seen to be common to all populations. I, instead, was hungry for something that grew from the very roots of the individual.

CHAPTER 6

FINDING THE ROOTS

During my residency I engaged as much as possible in the use of imagery in psychotherapy. I was continually intrigued by the power of the imagery to move toward a resolution of conflicts or an understanding of symptoms in a way that extended beyond the intellect. My early work in this area resulted in a book coauthored with Teresa Rennick, RN, entitled *Inner Journeys: Visualization in Growth and Therapy* (Turnstone Press, 1984).

At that time I had not yet differentiated between visualization and deep imagery. I presently see imagery as existing on three levels: The first level is visualization: imagery that is directed by someone else or by one's own thinking. This is the imagery that conforms to directions given from outside of imagery and is the dimension of imagery that most people know. ("Imagine that you are floating on a deep blue sea.")

The second is fantasy, imagery that fulfills unmet needs and hopes; fantasy is the imagery that fills most daydreams. Fantasy fulfills a yearning but also perpetuates that yearning. It does not arrive at a viable resolution. In fantasy I see the woman I love or the champion I yearn to become and although there is a sense of satisfaction I am also aware that there is a falseness to it. It is only vicariously satisfying. Fantasy may be a way of approaching and avoiding at the same time.

The third is deep imagery. This imagery is discovered rather than invented. It comes spontaneously and has its own aliveness and its own direction, its own intelligence. It is imagery that we cannot control but we can interact with it and develop a relationship with it. It is the imagery that comes to us in dreams but it can also be invited forth during waking consciousness. And although the subtitle of my first book was *Visualization in Growth and Therapy* (1984) I was in fact working with deep imagery and I have been involved with it ever since.

My early involvement with imagery was fascinating but it always seemed piecemeal, dependent upon the orienting situation, and not having a sustaining fabric of its own. The theoretical models then available, Jung's archetypal psychology and Assagioli's Psychosynthesis were both heavily weighted in the social dimension, and seemed dependent upon the external application of the theory. I felt a need for something more personally rooted in the individual. I was soon to find it.

Following the completion of my residency in 1981, I resigned my position at the university, from which I had been on leave of absence for two years, and obtained part-time employment as a therapist in a small psychotherapy clinic. I was soon to discover the orientation that has occupied me ever since and which has provided the main orientation in my life and in my own healing and growing. It is an orientation which has come to be known as the *Personal Totem Pole Process* (Gallegos, 1990). The fabric from which it arises is the energy system of the body, primarily the alignment of the major energy centers known as the chakras, but, in fact, involving the entire energy system. This was the psychological substrate I had been intuitively searching for! The human energy system and deep imagery are the two sides of one coin. This is the link between the body and the mind!

What I discovered was that animals readily come forth out of the energies of the body, when viewed through the window of deep imagery. We are rooted in animals! Our deep imagination has always shown us animals. Children dream of animals more than anything else. And why not? It is from the energy of animals that each one of us has evolved. In fact, our energy is animal energy no matter how much we have tried to overlay it with thinking! In fact, the thoughts that we have about animals are not the animals but only thoughts, and so they follow the laws of thinking rather than the aliveness of animals.

The only way we can really know animals from the inside is to become specific animals through our imagery or to plunge into our own aliveness and to discover it first hand through direct experience. Our dreams have also always been full of animals and frequently animals appear spontaneously in our imagination, un-bidden, during our waking day.

If we invite an animal to come forth from a chakra the nature of the animal its condition and its circumstances depict the status of the energy from which it arises, e.g., if the energy is undeveloped the animal may appear as a young or newly born animal.

If the energy is restricted or contained the animal may appear in a cage or bound in some way. If the energy is suppressed the animal may be buried. If the energy is not flowing the animal may be dead or may not appear at all. If the energy is injured the animal will appear injured in some way. The energies can be viewed directly with no guesswork! Furthermore, the animals show us that these energies are alive, are living energies, each with its own intelligence and creativity!

The other fascinating things that became immediately evident was that these energies have a relationship with one another, and that this relationship is a healing relationship! These inner energies can come together to heal injured aspects of ourselves. And they undertake this healing naturally and spontaneously when we allow it.

Although I have described the circumstances of this discovery in *The Personal Totem Pole* (1990) I will include a shortened version of it here:

I was jogging one evening through the hills of the small town where I was living in southern Oregon. Iran eight miles every evening; four miles out from my doorstep up a set of hills and four miles back. As I was returning, just at dusk, I had the sudden vision that there was a bear in my heart and an eagle in my head, and I could feel and see them in those places in my body. As I continued jogging I realized that these two animals were in the areas known as the fourth and sixth chakras. I immediately thought to myself, "I wonder what my other chakra animals are?"

I focused in my body and I could see clearly that in my throat there was a winged white horse, in my solar plexus there was a stag, in my belly a whale, and at the base of my spine there was a rabbit. I was completely intrigued by this vision and by the obvious appropriateness of the animals in these places within me.

I had learned about the chakras from a sensitive and skillful therapist named Ma Prem Mala who had recently returned from India where she had been studying. She was a therapist who consistently brought clients to a sense of resolution at the end of each therapy session. Mala taught me that there were concentrations of energy located in different areas of the body. Seven of these energy centers are located along the body midline and each center is related to certain emotional or psychological functions or processes of action. Mala called these centers "chakras," a Sanskrit term meaning wheel. This ancient perspective describes the human being as composed of centers of energy which in the healthy individual are open and the energy is able to flow freely. However, if any of the centers is blocked the person will be incapable of efficiently utilizing the energy at that level, and will experience a certain deficiency or even physical illness. For a person to be healthy, both physically and psychologically, energy must flow freely through every chakra. And each chakra is related to a characteristic aspect of ones being.

She taught me that the first center (the grounding or root chakra) is located at the base of the spine in the middle of the perineum. Through the energy in this chakra a healthy person experiences a sense of security and a wholesome relationship to the earth and to nature. The second center is located just below the navel, in what the Japanese call the "hara," or what we call the belly. Its domain is the passions and emotions. When it is fully functional the person experiences a depth of feeling and is emotionally aware.

The third energy center is in the solar plexus and is related to one's personal power, not the typical Western view of power which is viewed as control, force, or coercion, but the power to act, cleanly, deliberately and effectively. The fourth is centered in the heart and is concerned with love and compassion. The fifth is in the throat and is the power of expression. The sixth is located in the forehead and is sometimes known as the "third eye". It is related to the intellect and intuition. The seventh, the crown chakra, is located at the very top of the head, and is concerned with the relationship to one's spirit.

Because of my extensive training in science and Behaviorism I was originally skeptical of this view. My tendency was to ask, "What is it really?" , and try to envision these centers in terms of underlying neural plexuses or glandular systems: something objective that I could be comfortable with. But I soon understood that the chakra system emanates from a subjective knowledge of the body, not an objective one. This knowledge came not from an outer knowing but from an inner knowing.

After meeting these animals in my chakras I began wondering how the chakra system was related to a group of animals. What would be the animal equivalent of all chakras fully functioning in relation to each other? In the chakra system it would mean each chakra being open and healthy, fully processing its energy, and allowing this energy to flow freely between all chakras. For the animals I had the sense that this would entail all the animals being fully free and healthy, and living in harmony and open communication with each other. So I went to each of my animals and asked if they would meet together with one another. They all willingly agreed and at once gathered together under a large old Live Oak tree.

I was surprised to see that few of them had met before. As they gathered they formed a circle. The rabbit looked at the others and immediately began telling them how small and weak he felt in their presence, how afraid he was of them because they were all large and powerful, and how he felt he should not be part of that group.

As the rabbit spoke a memory came to me of something I had not thought about in forty years! I was five years old. I had been in kindergarten for several weeks. The kindergarten class had consisted of a dozen children and we met in a large comfortable and sunny room. As my mother was a teacher I had been well prepared for school. I could already read a few words and I knew how to count. I had friends in this class. The class was relaxed and the teacher was gentle and understanding.

However, this suddenly came to an end when one day the teacher came over to me and said, "You're too smart to be in kindergarten. You really should be in the first grade." She took me by the arm and led me down a long hallway to the first grade classroom opened the door and ushered me inside. There were thirty-first graders sitting in rows and they were all bigger and older than I. I was put in an empty seat in one of the long neat rows of desks. I felt an immediate panic and wanted to leave. I knew I did not belong here at all. I was much too small and incompetent!

As the memory ran through my mind I realized that this feeling had been with me all my life, especially in new situations where there were people I did not know. A feeling of panic, of not belonging, of not being as strong or as competent as the other people there. And it was a feeling that I had felt but the originating circumstances had been absent from my awareness through all of my schooling including my PhD program and my job as a professor! And so I presumed that the feeling had originated in the present circumstance rather than being only a feeling memory.

After the rabbit had spoken the whale (from my belly) turned to the rabbit and said, "You do belong here! You are one of us!" Then each animal in turn addressed the rabbit and told it how much it was appreciated and loved. They assured it that it was one of them and that it belonged with them. The rabbit was deeply touched by their kindness and acceptance.

They all offered their support and urged the rabbit to grow to be their equal. At this the rabbit suddenly began growing larger and larger until it was a giant rabbit about eight feet tall. The other animals stood back in appreciation. The rabbit was now very still and settled, no longer afraid, and with a deep sense of belonging.

I was amazed to observe all this! As the rabbit was growing I personally experienced my old feeling of not belonging, of being small and weak, drain away and leave me. This intense emotion that had been with me for over forty years was now suddenly gone!

I felt a sense of ease and settled-ness that I had never before experienced. And I felt a deep appreciation for the rabbit and for the support the other animals had offered it.

I was deeply moved by the significance of what I had encountered: an inner system that shows us our injuries, even when we have been unaware of the injury for the greatest part of our lives, and spontaneously initiates the healing of the injury. It does this quickly, gently and with a sense of natural ease. This was the inner healing system that I had been searching for all my life

CHAPTER 7

QUESTIONS

This discovery of the chakra animals was profound for me. On the one hand I was elated that I had finally encountered a way to heal and grow that was independent of someone else's theory of who I was or how I should be. This in itself was tremendously refreshing! It was an orientation that was somehow designed around me: around who I am, around what happened to me, around the pace and the sequence of what it is I need to work with in order to go through the healing of injuries which I didn't even know existed. It was the vehicle that I had been searching for all my life. It was not dependent upon me following someone else's ideas or orders. Discovering it felt like being freed from a cage, from a prison, and felt like the beginning of a return to what was natural for me. It soon became apparent to me that the chakra animals knew much better than I did who I originally was (or am), what happened to me that I came to be different from who I am, and how to bring me to the experiences that are essential for my return to who I originally am.

Additionally, in using this approach with the clients in the therapy center, I became aware of how powerful and essential the animals were for the healing of other people. I knew I had never before met anything so specifically powerful in healing the lives of people who had been emotionally injured.

This was effective not only in cases of emotional injury, but also in cases of headache, asthma, painful menstrual periods, and healing the recovery from surgery. Here was an approach that brought the individual more into a healthy alignment with who that individual really was regardless of what might have happened to the person along the route of their life. I felt the power of this approach so vitally that one of my concerns was that I might die before this approach had made its way out into the world, so I began presenting talks, demonstrations, workshops, and trainings about this work wherever and whenever I could.

One of the beautiful things about training others in this work was that I myself could journey to meet with my own animals within the context of the training. And curiously, this had a variety of effects. On the one hand I could do my own healing and growing while I was in the process of training others and this is what I had been seeking all my life.

Secondly, the people I was training were amazed that I would essentially allow myself to be one of them, to go through my own process along with them, rather than playing the role of teacher. This also had the effect of making it clear to them that it was not me that was in charge of the process, but that the process from which these chakra animals arose and the patterns that they follow was a deeper dimension within me, and within each of them, if they would only allow themselves to be guided by this deeper dimension rather than feeling that they were somehow in charge of it.

The Personal Totem Pole approach also continued to lead me deeper and deeper into other dimensions of healing and growing. Since this inner dimension is so naturally healing a question that began to occupy me at this time is why are we so injured? If we carry within ourselves this remarkable healing dimension why do we spend so much of our lives injured?

The answer began to make itself known gradually, and still does. For one thing, this process requires our awareness, our support, and our interaction with it. It is not autonomous although it is independent. That is to say, it has its own way of going about things, it has its own intelligence, and its own aliveness that is beyond our control. We are not in control of it nor were we intended to be. However, it does require our participation!

And we have learned to withdraw our support and our participation from this dimension, through the mistaken stories that we were told about it and that we tell about it, but also, because historically and socially, we have been deeply injured in that relationship. We have developed an erroneous understanding of this inner dimension and we have also become so outer oriented that there is little social support for turning back inward.

We have, for whatever reason, deliberately turned away from the natural healing aspect of who we each are. Each one of us is a healer, and we are each particularly a healer of our own selves. How could we ever have become so disconnected from such an essential and remarkable dimension of who we are? How and why did we ever become so disoriented?

CHAPTER 8

DISCOVERING FEELING

In 1984, I decided, together with my wife and young daughter, to move to Lexington, Massachusetts, a suburb of Boston, where I opened a private psychotherapy practice. There I successfully introduced clients to the Personal Totem Pole Process. I was fascinated by the fact that here in the super sophisticated city of Boston and its suburbs the chakra animals were just as effective as they had been in rural Oregon where my clients had known almost nothing about therapy. In Lexington most of my clients had already been to a number of therapists and some were therapists themselves, but upon introducing them to the chakra animals, long sought healings began to take place. Our stay in Lexington lasted for fourteen months.

But as my then wife, Kay, was born in California and I in New Mexico, we missed the West. So we made arrangements to move to California. Jeannette Samanen, a good friend who was also a therapist, offered me her practice in Palo Alto as her husband was taking a new position in Pennsylvania and they would soon be moving.

My wife made the arrangements for our move, rented a trailer which I would pull with our van and began packing our belongings in it. She and our daughter would fly to California to spend Christmas with her parents and I would complete the packing and drive out to meet them there arriving several days before Christmas. All went well. We purchased coach flight tickets and were able to upgrade them to first class with my frequent flyer miles. On the day they were to leave I drove them to Logan Airport and carried my two-year old daughter onto the plane.

After I had buckled her into her seat next to my wife I turned to leave and she realized for the first time that I wouldn't be coming with them. She held out her arms to me, her eyes full of tears, and cried, "No, Daddy, don't go!" I felt a deep pang of sadness, explained to her that I would come later with our belongings, and left the plane. As I walked off of the plane and drove home my sadness was very deep. I had the feeling that I would never see my wife and daughter again.

Arriving at our house I walked into my office and sat in an easy chair and cried and cried. I sat there until long past midnight and then went to bed. I awoke early in the morning, still feeling that great sadness and loss, and again sat in the chair in my office unable to do anything else.

I was very concerned about the extent of my sadness. I called my wife at her parents' house in California. They had arrived well. I told her about my extreme sadness and she offered to return to Boston but I knew that was not a solution. For several days I moped around, mostly just sat in the chair in my office and felt this deep, almost despairing sadness. I was unable to pack and barely ate.

And then suddenly one evening as I was sitting in the chair just feeling that awesome sadness I suddenly became aware that the feeling dimension of me was an intact being. Not that it was separate from me but that it had its own unity, its own organization, its own integrity. It was an experiential entity in and of itself! As I suddenly saw it in such a light I realized that all my life I had treated it as if it were something mechanical, as if it could be manipulated and dictated to, as if one aspect of it could be brought forth and another aspect discarded, as if it were nothing other than a series of components that could be replaced or moved around at my whim. I saw that there were aspects of it that I had hated, terror, for example, which I interpreted as cowardice. And others, like anger and rage, that I had feared. I had never understood that feeling was an aspect of me that had its own integrity and its own way of being, like a hand whose fingers all work in coordination with one another.

"I feel so bad about the way I have treated you!" I said to it. "Yes, you have treated me badly," it replied.

"I've acted as if you didn't know what you were doing and I was in charge of you!" I said. "Yes, that is how you have been with me," it said.

I was struck by how nonjudgmental its comments were. It spoke to me with equanimity and balance, not the anger and retribution that one would expect from a being that had been mistreated and misunderstood all its life. No. Not misunderstood, for there was no attempt to understand it. I had treated it as if its own existence were not even worth considering and as if it was there to do my own bidding. I had missed the fact that its existence had a value all its own, and a meaning that was beyond the intellectual meaning I had seen it through. I cried and cried at how totally unaware I had been of its existence and how in my ignorance I had treated it so brutally. I apologized to it over and over again. "I feel so sorry about the way I have treated you!"

"Yes, you treated me badly!" , was its reply.

I sat with it through Christmas, still amazed at my lack of awareness of this dimension of myself and of how I should have given it not only my respect but also my trust and understanding.

The day after Christmas I was sitting with it, again apologizing profusely. I felt like a jail guard who suddenly discovers that he has been treating the prisoners cruelly and without any consideration for their own being while having thought all along that this is the way one treats such people. "I am so sorry for the way I have treated you!"

"Yes, but it has not been so bad," it replied, "for after all it did eventually bring us back together. Now, let's get going! I'll help you pack!"

I stood up, packed boxes and loaded them into the trailer until after midnight, awoke early the next morning and continued packing and left in the late afternoon. I felt energized and focused, together like I had never been before. I drove and drove until I arrived in St. Louis around eleven the following night. I pulled into a parking area, crawled onto the futon that was in the van and fell soundly asleep.

In the middle of the night I sat up abruptly out of a deep sleep. The words were still ringing in my ear. "Now it's time for you to die!" I was stunned. I didn't know if the words had come from a dream but they filled my mind and I was vitally awake. Two things came prominently to mind. "But there are things I still want to do before I die! I would like to be around to take care of my daughter and I would also like to see my work (with the chakra animal imagery) make its way into the world."

"Right now you are only a memory in your daughters mind," the voice said. "She is with people that love her and if you were to die right now it would be an easy transition for her. And your work will continue on through the people you have introduced it to, perhaps even spurred on by your death."

The reply made sense and I could understand the logic of what I was being told. "What would it be like if I die?" I asked. I then felt myself being whisked off into the cosmos, further and further, beyond the sun, beyond our solar system, beyond the Milky Way. And even further until I was on the edge of the universe, and still further until I was at such a vantage point that I could see the universe in its entirety. I was stunned by what I saw: the universe was alive! And it was a single organism of awesome complexity, but whole and totally integrated. I recognized that it was still in the stage of its early development, comparable to a fetus, still differentiating the various aspects of itself. I saw how everything that exists, including me and every being was a part of that awesome being. We were aspects of its components just like the various parts of our own being are aspects of who we are. I saw that everything that exists is part of a greater whole and that the whole requires every part in order to be fully who it is. Every part is essential. And out of this a harmony ensues.

I then found myself saying, "If I have any choice in the matter I choose not to die right now." "Okay then. Let's get on the road!", the voice said. I found myself moving to the driver's seat and beginning to drive. It was 4 AM.

The profound and mysterious complexity of the Universe accompanies me to this day, its unity, its aliveness, and the impossibility of ever expressing it in words haunts me. Every aspect of the Universe, including us, has a place of relationship with it. We are perhaps the only beings who think that we are somehow independent, not realizing that our most profound task is to remain aligned with the Universe, in relationship with this awesome, vast being. And that our own wholeness is vital for the wholeness of the Universe. And only in this way do we ultimately come to experience our own place of belonging in the Universe.

CHAPTER 9

DIFFERENT WAYS OF KNOWING

My work with the chakra animals was also soon to plunge me into a new orientation. It revolved around the question that many philosophers have dealt with: how do we know? How does knowing happen? What are the passageways through which knowing takes place? It brought me ultimately to a serious questioning of what for me, scholastically, had been the limitations of our modern culturally approved ways of knowing: through thinking and through science.

In 1986, while searching for a comprehensible way of presenting the chakra animals to a group of people who wished to be trained in working with this process, I was led to the four ways of knowing. I felt I should begin by comparing imagery to our other ways of knowing. But how does deep imagery differ from our other ways of knowing, and, fundamentally, what are our other ways of knowing?

Of course there is thinking on which we spend so much of our school time. Then there is sensing, the aspect through which we directly know the world around (seeing, hearing, touching, tasting and smelling). I was also aware that feeling was a way of knowing, although we seem to have great difficulty articulating what it is that is known through feeling. My subsequent experience with these ways of knowing resulted in a book called Animals of the Four Windows: Integrating Thinking, Sensing, Feeling, and Imagery (Gallegos, 1991).

Just as the chakra animals had come forth out of the major energy centers, these animals readily came forth out of the four modes of knowing: thinking, sensing, feeling and imagery. I was amazed at how stupendously dynamic these animals were. They immediately began teaching me about themselves and correcting wrong assumptions I had held, healing aspects of themselves (and of me) that had been injured, and interacting with one another in order to come into a more integrated state of wholeness with one another.

Interestingly, my first visit to the animals of the four ways of knowing was preceded by an intense dream:

DREAM: NIGHT OF FEB 27-28, 1987

I was on an expedition with several other people. We had arrived at the top of a mountain where there was not a mountain peak but a bowl-like depression. It was extremely cold at this altitude. In the depression we were awed to discover an extremely large sabre-tooth tiger and a strong mule or donkey, both frozen and mummified, apparently long ago.

The tiger was on its back with the large sabre teeth sticking up in the air. The two animals seemed to have killed each other in battle, or fought to a stalemate in which they both froze.

That afternoon I retired to a room where I knew I wouldn't be disturbed. I relaxed on a couch, and called forth within myself for the animals of the four ways of knowing.

The first animal that appeared was an ant, going along a relatively straight line, stopping to touch each other ant that it met, very limited and one-dimensional. I felt immediately that this was my animal for thinking. Then suddenly the eagle from my forehead chakra appeared, swooped down and ate the ant. I was completely surprised. Eagle had been the first chakra animal ever to appear to me. I suddenly realized that Eagle is also the animal of my thinking and that the ant was the way I had been thinking about thinking! My thinking is much more direct, clear, and powerful than I had previously realized, and the eagle told me that it was he who was responsible for the success of the imagery work I have been doing. He told me that it is through thinking that I am able to communicate about the animals in the first place, it is through thinking that I first knew to look for the other animals in the chakras and it is because of thinking that I have met the rest of the animals. Eagle told me that I must learn to respect thinking more, and to realize the vastness of the dimensions it can enter.

I had been confusing thinking with the wrongful way I had been educated. I soon began to understand that thinking is deeply organic and intelligent and that education distorts thinking by requiring that we imitate other people's thinking rather than nurturing and respecting our own. Thinking becomes a dancing bear, responding to other people's questions rather than remaining in its own natural pace and rhythms.

Proper education should help the student learn about and understand his own way of thinking, not to imitate someone else's thought. The thinking part of who we are is brilliant and can learn anything, but we are taught many things that go directly against the natural wholeness of our own being.

We must also understand that thinking works differently from our other three ways of knowing. It must be respected for the way it works and it must not be expected to mirror the ways that sensing, feeling, and imagery work. Each way of knowing has its own particular specialty, must be allowed to work in its own way, and must be understood within that dynamic.

Thinking first of all is heavily language dependent! It requires a set of signs and symbols that we generally agree upon and which also serve as our common means of communication. And the particular language that we learn imposes its own structure on the surface of our thinking.

Thinking was not meant to be a dictator. Thinking broadens and deepens itself by learning from our other modes of knowing, but it was never intended to be their boss. Thinking must have patience and allow room for deeper processes. Our education system hardly promotes this. We have come to think that thinking is a process of identifying facts, but thinking actually is founded in storytelling. Our earliest learning is communicated through stories; the bard was the original teacher!

Thinking also works by focusing our awareness on differences but also by capturing those differences into generalizations, allowing us to both see how things are different and how they are similar. But because of one particular propensity, polarization, we frequently come to be lodged in only one end of a difference. One pole of a concept gains its identity through differentiating itself from its opposite pole. In other words, we become stuck in only one end of our thinking. And not realizing we are stuck anywhere (thinking we are living in "the truth") we then assign the opposite of the place we are stuck to another location or to other people.

And we can readily do this for several reasons, which can include:

1. We gather together with other people who are similarly polarized,
2. It becomes uncomfortable to embrace both sides of a polarity, primarily because of a rather rigid sense of identity that we have learned to hold (which itself is also one end of a polarization),
3. We have learned to live in our intentions (or anticipations or expectations) rather than in the fullness of the present moment (intention involves holding a rigid focus on the outcome, which is itself a narrowing of awareness),
4. We are unaware of the nature of our knowing through feeling and this allows the attribution to others of an experience that belongs to us, commonly known as projection.

For generations we have focused outward and not inward. Because of this we have become exceedingly ignorant about our own inner being, that is, we have learned to deliberately ignore those ways of knowing that require an inward focus. And without this inward focus we attribute much more credence to thinking as a way of knowing without being aware of the pitfalls of such an orientation. In fact, we are usually unaware of the fact that we are even thinking and come to confuse our own creation (i.e., the stories we tell ourselves) with The Creation (the beauty and immensity of our God-given Universe, ourselves included!).

Additionally, through the way thinking was misused on us when we were children, we ourselves have come to use thinking for giving ourselves instructions and directions rather than for describing to ourselves what is happening in our awareness and in our experience.

Perhaps the most damaging aspect of thinking is that we have come to think that understanding is the endpoint of our living. Once we understand something then we can relax. Whereas not thinking but experiencing (including the experience of thinking) is our ultimate encounter with aliveness. It is this realization that led Lao Tsu to write the Tao Te Ching.

I have ultimately come to see that perhaps the most profound aspect of thinking emerges in storytelling; thinking reaches its pinnacle in the telling of stories. Knowing through sensing is originally the most thoroughly used way of knowing. I say originally because we have come to live in such a synthetic environment that sensing has been displaced by thinking. And we have arrived at a place where what we sense is interpreted, and where the major part of our world has come to be a human social world.

Originally, and when we are newborn, the senses loom large. Every baby faces the world in such an open eyed way, seeing, looking all around, recognizing, finding safety in the familiar and being intrigued by the unfamiliar. Our hearing is also open and curious, but here we encounter an assaultive amount of coaching: we are bombarded by the sounds called words, those sounds made by other humans, and in our American culture in particular, sounds that people have come to believe are essential for social interconnection. Also, our sense of smell, of taste, and of touch are vital for our knowing of this new world. This way of knowing, through the senses, in me had retreated so far that it came forth as a jellyfish. Now a jellyfish is a beautiful animal in its natural setting: in the ocean beneath the water. Here one sees its soft and subtle delicate structure, its beautiful fluidity and balance, its transparency. But out of the ocean, out of its natural habitat, it appears to be a formless blob of jelly, without structure, without the ability to move on its own, and without any apparent differentiation.

I was also shown that my feeling dimension had been divided and severely polarized. I was taken there by my eagle. We landed in a jungle and an elephant immediately appeared, charging directly toward me and trumpeting loudly. He was large and powerful, charging at me with tremendous speed. In fact, his momentum was so great that he couldn't stop when he reached me and it carried him about ten feet beyond me. The elephant kept trumpeting in anguish, as if he were in agony. I was surprised at his power. I knew this was my knowing through feeling.

Eagle urged me to become the elephant. After some initial hesitation I agreed and merged into the elephant. I was immediately shocked to realize how much pain the elephant was in. Its entire body was filled with pain. I also realized what a powerful animal it was. I became aware of its heaviness, its solidness, the capacity of its tusks, and its relatively thick skin. While I was inside it the elephant began stomping the ground and smashing trees. Then suddenly my father appeared and the elephant picked him up and smashed him into the ground.

With this it became more settled and I then realized that its front legs were hobbled. I was also aware of how invaded it had been, and that most of the damage was done to this animal during my childhood. It was an animal that could know very sensitively by means of its trunk and could also hear keenly with its large ears.

I emerged from it and unlocked and removed the hobble and salved its legs. They were worn and sore where the hobble had been. It lifted its left front leg and I saw there was a thorn in it.

As I examined it more closely I realized that it wasn't a thorn but a spike that was deeply embedded. It had been deliberately driven into its foot. I extracted the spike and put some salve on the wound. The elephant lay down and I tended it fully, taking care first of its feet, then washing and scrubbing it all over, drying it and polishing its tusks and nails. It was only then that I became aware it was a female elephant, although it had been trumpeting like a bull elephant.

Then I suddenly found myself on a camel. I thought that perhaps the elephant had transformed into a camel, but I saw the elephant was still there, lying on its side and not looking well. The camel was rather shy but very enduring. It carried me regally. It was strong and it moved with relative precision and dignity. I became aware of it as a pack animal in caravans and of how camels initially resist being loaded with their burdens. It seemed that one of its main modes of responding was resistance and withdrawal. I became aware of my own tendency to withdraw from relationships. I thought about the way I resisted my father's demands when I was a child, although outwardly conforming. I climbed down off of it and brushed it with a curry comb. The camel was a male.

The eagle suggested that the camel and the elephant merge. The elephant was initially reluctant to do so, but it eventually agreed. They merged into one another and suddenly a tiger appeared in their place. Eagle then suggested that I become the tiger. As I merged into the tiger's body I became aware of how unified it was. Its entire body could feel exactly what was happening around it. Whereas the bodies of both the elephant and the camel seemed to be differentiated into certain specializations, the tiger on the other hand was agile, multicolored, stealthy; it could creep silently, climb trees, wait in stillness, spring powerfully. It had powerful shoulders and keen senses. It was at home in the jungle, and it was dominated by no one. It felt good. I appreciated the way in which the camel and elephant had been essential for my survival, and the tiger felt like a worthy inheritor of their abilities, adding its own quality of tremendous integration. (Gallegos 1991)

Because of a misunderstanding about feeling as a way of knowing we have not allowed ourselves to fully enter into feeling. We hold many thoughts about feeling and feelings, we give ourselves directions about what we should feel and why, but we are usually ignorant about the knowing that feeling allows us. This ignorance comes from certain beliefs or stories that we maintain about what is real. In fact, feeling is our way of knowing energy directly. The energies that we ourselves are and the energies that emanate from the world and from the universe. We have been taught that each thing around us is an object and this gets in the way of experiencing the energies that these objects also are. Feeling is the knowing of energies directly.

For some reason we have had difficulty acknowledging the body as a general energy receptor even though we have no problem in recognizing that the body has specialized in the reception of specific kinds of energy through the development of the five senses. These areas of specialization, these senses, could not have arisen if the body were not a general energy receptor to begin with.

The body receives energies and these received energies are experienced as feelings. Our feelings are the knowing of energies directly. But since our body also creates energies (we do call some of these energies "emotions," i.e. motions that we emit) we must also become fully aware of the feelings that arise within us in order to be able to distinguish between the energies that reach us from the outside and the energies that arise within us. This problem, that we are the knowers of external energies and also the creators of energies, has caused much confusion. We have not learned to differentiate between the energies that reach us from the external world and the energies that we generate individually. Some people assume responsibility for energies that they do not create and others deny responsibility for the energies that they create. Most of us create energies automatically when external energies reach us (responding to anger with anger, for example) and rationalize our own creation by blaming it on the external event. One of the beautiful aspects of growing and maturing is the development of the ability to respond to an external energy with our own inner creation in a transformative way.

We live in such a limited environment, limited to the nuclear family or to others of similar age, that we have few opportunities to experience and to express abroad range of energies. Another confounding factor is that most of us grew up in situations where certain energies were either not allowed or completely denied. We have also not learned to differentiate between experiencing an energy and putting that energy into action. And feeling is a way of knowing that is so different from thinking that we have almost polarized it into nonexistence.

In fact, the energy that we are was once known as "spirit," and in the modern age we have become so disconnected from this spirit of who we are, replacing it with an identity, that we can hardly be thought to be spiritual, i.e., energized. We must feel the energy of our aliveness in order to be fully whole!

Eagle then flew me to an immense dragon, my knowing through imagery. It was just emerging from having been buried in the earth. Entire villages and landscapes adhered to the surface of its body as it emerged from the earth. As it shook them off, I realized that it had carried upon itself all of everything. Imagery is the foundation. Any world we envision is carried by imagery. It precedes all. It carries all. Even knowing through sensing has little persistence, is fleeting and delicate, like the jellyfish. It is imagery that connects it all together and gives it presence and persistence. The dragon was tremendous, immensely alive. I never did see it all, as the rest of it was covered with the outer world. The dragon asked only that I respect it. I do.

I then wanted to explore the relationship between all these animals and see how they got along together, but the eagle indicated that it was not time yet for that, and it would have to be done on another occasion. The following day I went again to meet with these animals. Eagle (thinking) took me first to the dragon (imagery), who was emerging from the encrustation of all that he had carried on his surface. He was very alive and serpentine. I was surprised that this was the first one Eagle would take me to, and even more surprised that he then took me to the jellyfish(sensing). Jellyfish came over to Dragon. Dragon seemed intimidated by the jellyfish, at first retreating from it. Jellyfish then latched onto Dragon and eventually engulfed Dragon. Dragon felt honored, as if it had returned to its natural relationship with Jellyfish, who was now a fine, thin luminous sheath enveloping Dragon. They had become one indefinable creature. Dragon was totally at home as the core of Jellyfish and seemed to give Jellyfish some real substance. (Gallegos 1991)

Imagery provides us with the inner knowing of everything that exists. Our sensing presents the knowing of the outside of objects, our feeling allows us the knowing of the energies of objects, our thinking allows us to conceptualize and tell stories, but our imagery allows us the knowing of the inner aspects. And this knowing of the inner is vital when it comes to knowing ourselves. Without it we cease to know the remarkable depths and brilliance of our inner being.

The path of deep imagery is a path that has been misunderstood and misinterpreted, and a path that has been followed by very few even though it is so readily available to everyone. The path of deep imagery is a path whose knowing includes a knowing of healing, of gathering the disparate parts of oneself together again, of filling out those potentials that have not yet come into being, and of bringing all of these dimensions together into a single whole. We have longed for that wholeness our entire lives and the path toward it has always been available in the deepest parts of who we are!

CHAPTER 10

HEALING JOURNEYS

I plunged into working with deep imagery like a man lost in the desert who has just discovered an oasis. I was thrilled by the discovery of the fact that this dimension knew me so intimately, yet was so gentle, so knowing of my own pace. But there was also a ferociousness in it. It would plunge me into experiences that were startling, almost overwhelming, pushing me through the synthetic boundaries that had been built up during my lifetime. I understood that I had been a creature needing to survive but I was also starving to grow. Survival was not an adequate goal in my life, although it had been a necessary condition. And my actions, beliefs, feelings, outward orientation had been structured as a means of survival. It was predictable, rigid, and encasing. I was trapped within the things I had learned to do to survive, and my hunger was for a greater realm, the realm that was my true potential. And in order for me to grow my survival mode had to die.

I was taken through many deaths. In fact, each change involved a kind of death, the death of the perspective that I had maintained up to that point. But there was also the fact of dying that held so much terror for me. I had grown up in a culture where there was such an intense focus on the body, the appearance of the body, the actions of the body, the behavior of the body, and I had to be shown that the body was not the ideas that I had learned about it.

Ultimately the body is like a womb, or like a doorway. It is the means of passage by which we come forth into this greater realm. I was also shown over and over again the way in which my thinking had been calcified, had become predictable, not living its own creativity but available to whoever wanted to test its knowing and its memory. My thinking had become a slave to others rather than the participant in the journey of this being that I am in all of my complexity. My understanding had to arrive at an acceptance of the fact that I am a multitudinous being with innumerable facets, many of them quite mysterious, rather than the predictable machine I had been raised to believe I should be.

My initial journeys were with the chakra animals. I was deeply moved by the support they gave me primarily in their consistent presence. I felt myself to be supported from within. I could consult with them when I had questions or doubts. Sometimes they would answer in words and thoughts but mostly they would take me through some kind of an experience.

For example, while driving to Salem, Oregon, to take my oral exam for licensure as a therapist, I went to each animal and asked if it would support me during the exam. Every animal answered that it would, but when I came to my throat animal I saw that it had changed from a white horse to a beautiful golden horse and I felt a deep warmth within me. I had the feeling that I would be able to express myself beautifully. And I did. Following the exam I was sent out of the room while the examiners consulted among themselves. They taped their comments and gave me a copy of the tape which I listened to on the way home. Their comments were all laudatory and one of them even remarked that if he was going to go into therapy he would want a therapist as warm and as mature as I was. I felt a deep elation and I knew it was the inner support of the animals that had been responsible for this.

I came more and more to recognize the remarkable creatures that we are, each one of us, and the profound aliveness that exists in each one of us far beyond the aliveness that we take for granted. A deep aliveness that is awesomely creative. An aliveness whose veracity we have discounted or ignored because it doesn't fit into our Western cultural theory. Whenever an animal would go through a change or a transformation I experienced its significance deep within myself. It was a communication that changed me by its very existence, like the slap of a Zen master.

For example, there was a period of time when my heart animal had become four pastel colored flowers. They never spoke but just waved in the wind, bending in the winds direction. I was intrigued by them. They were present for many months and then one day there was only one flower but it looked strange: it was quite dense and purple, with only two petals, and again it would not respond to me in anyway. Then on one occasion I was guiding a group of people to meet their heart animals and while they were journeying I went to my own heart to see what was going on in myself.

Again, this dense, strange purple flower appeared which intrigued me so. But suddenly the eagle from my forehead appeared, its beak opened wide and a shaman leaned forth out of the beak. The shaman held a spear in his hand. With a mighty move he heaved the spear down toward the flower. The spear entered the water (I had not previously noticed the water) and I heard a roar as a large whale came up out of the water. The whale came forth very angry as the shaman laughed and laughed. The strange flower had been the tale of this whale and the shaman had heaved a harpoon, not a spear, at it. I then understood that my heart had been very passive when it should have been rightfully angry about a certain situation with my wife!

The shaman continued to appear spontaneously from time to time. On one occasion when I was having some questions about the realm of shamanism in the work I was doing he appeared and told me, "You are not a shaman, so don't worry about it! I am the shaman. I will take care of whatever needs to be taken care of!" This relieved me of any concern with shamanism and allowed me to focus on just being a therapist leading people to the deep organic imagery that is natural to everyone.

At another period of time all of my animals, one by one, became elements in the landscape. My solar plexus was a large waterfall, my grounding element was the earth, my crown element was the sky. My belly was a forest, my heart a lake. This coincided with a time of really coming to feel at home in the world.

More recently my animals are very flexible, that is, I never know who is going to be where, but they are always appropriate to the situation in which I find myself. Several of the animals, however, are quite stable and predictable: Eagle in my forehead, Bear in my heart, and Whale in my eighth chakra, about afoot above my head. I didn't know the eighth chakra even existed until I was at a Transpersonal Psychology conference where Gay Luce led the group into an experience of the eighth chakra. It is the chakra that connects the individual to the universe.

The whale in my eighth chakra swims through the universe but sometimes the whale contains the universe within itself. Whale is large and powerful and very present.

For the most part, however, I allow the deep imagination to choose who will be sent to me and I enter into the relationship in total trust, knowing from long experience that the animals or guides that come are brilliant and know exactly what the experience is into which they will lead me.

Step by step, over many years, I have been changed from the inside. And as my inside changed I came to see the world differently. What follows are a few selected journeys that were involved in some of those changes.

CHAPTER 11

THE LYNX

When training a new group of therapists in imagery I frequently startle them by telling them that my growing comes first. Even though I am there to train them, my growing has to come first. I can only help someone grow as far as I have grown. That is not to say that they can't grow farther than I have, they certainly can, but as far as my help goes, I can only help them go as far as I have gone.

When I meet a therapist who gives his all to the client, at his own expense, I know I am looking at a person whose identity is closely interwoven with that of the client, and that real inter-dependencies will develop. I try to help my trainees understand that to be a therapist implies helping the client come into his or her own independence, and that includes independence from the therapist. This requires that the therapist also be a person who has achieved his or her own independence.

People are naturally social, especially once they have come into their wholeness, so there is no need to train them to be social. What we can do is to nurture and support their coming into their wholeness so their own natural social nature can be fully present.

When working with a group of trainees I also undertake my own work within the group. Some of them think that this implies a great trust of them. I do trust them. I also know that the animals are in charge. The process of returning to full relationship with one's imagery is completely trustworthy so long as one is willing to truthfully and directly relate to it. So I have no compunctions about engaging in my own process before the group. I expect them to do this in front me and in front of each other, why should I not also?

Some years ago I was teaching a class that met on weekends. We began our meeting in the evening by sitting in a circle and passing the talking staff. We all knew each other quite well since we had been meeting for over a year. There were twelve people in the class and we met once a month. At this initial talking staff council people spoke about what had been happening in their lives since we had last met.

After the talking staff had gone around the circle I asked who would like to journey. There was no reply and so I volunteered myself although I had no agenda, absolutely nothing that I felt I needed to work on. I know from the large amount of journeywork I have done that having no agenda is a very powerful place to be; one is open to everything.

I asked who in the group felt like guiding me. This is another thing: I trust them to know if this would be appropriate for them to do at this time. I don't think anything should be forced. If there are reasons they should not guide at a particular time they need to learn to trust this knowing in themselves just as readily as they should trust if it is appropriate for them to guide.

One of the women in the class offered to guide me. I lay on the floor in the middle of the circle, my guide sitting beside me. She guided me through a beautiful relaxation and then she suggested, "Call out and ask if there's an animal that needs to come meet with you."

Since the dimension of deep imagery itself knows us better than we know ourselves, one of the ways of proceeding after one has met the chakra animals and the animals of the four windows, is just to allow them to decide which of them needs to come and guide us. Rather than us deciding who we need to meet with and what needs to happen, we come to the place of trusting them, having already seen how beautifully they know how to bring about the experiences that we need for our healing or growing.

I called out within myself, "Is there an animal that needs to come meet with me at this time? If so, would you please come forth?" Immediately a lynx appeared, sitting beside me. I had never seen a lynx in my imagery before. Its eyes were bright and I particularly noticed the point of its ears. I asked lynx if it was my guide and it said yes.

"Lynx," I said, "what needs to happen here?" With no hesitation Lynx replied, "Follow me!" then turned around and began climbing a mountain that was just behind him. Lynx bounded up the mountain with great ease and I followed as closely as I could. I was climbing on all fours. The mountain was rocky, made of sharp, craggy boulders and it was not an easy climb. Lynx finally reached the top and sat at the very pinnacle of this sharp mountain. I arrived and sat just below him.

"What needs to happen now?" I asked.

"Keep climbing!" Lynx replied without hesitation.

I climbed until I was sitting on Lynx's head. "What now?" I asked.

I was truly mystified by what was going on. "Lower yourself into my body and look through my eyes," replied Lynx. I found myself moving slowly down until I occupied Lynx's body. As I looked through his eyes I was quite startled at what I saw. The mountain, which to me had been sharp, craggy, and dangerous, to Lynx was rubbery and trampoline-like, and was fun and bouncy.

The open space around, instead of being clear and transparent, shimmered in rainbow-like colors. I understood that this was the energy of the sky. The lynx sees the sky's energy whereas I just see its transparency.

"Now look at my body," said Lynx.

I looked at Lynx's body and again was surprised at what I saw. The body was not a material substance but was radiant, glowing, and the glow extended beyond what I would have taken to be the physical boundaries of the lynx's body.

I then found myself out of Lynx's body once more, sitting beside and slightly below him. "Wow," I said. "You see the world very differently from the way I see it!"

"That's because you're dead!" Lynx answered.

I was shocked. This was not at all what I expected to hear. Taken by surprise, I could only make a stunned reply. "I don't want to be dead! How did I die?"

"You killed yourself!"

"How did I kill myself?" I asked, incredulous at what I was hearing.

"Every time you avoided your fear you killed a little part of yourself!", answered Lynx in his straightforward manner.

Lynx then showed me my life from the beginning. An entire panorama of memories from my childhood began passing in review before my eyes. My avoidance of fear began in my childhood with the whippings and beatings my father gave me. I became terrified of him and avoided him as much as I could. I feared his criticism, his castigation, the hard look in his eye, his distrust, and I never knew when he was going to punish me. Every day was filled with situations where I did what I could to avoid him.

When I couldn't avoid him I avoided any responsibility that might result in a whipping. I learned to lie and be deceitful. This began a crystallization of my life that looked like the formation of a mineral crystal, with new accretions forming with each new avoidance, limiting my flexibility and my aliveness. Lynx showed me that I had also become afraid of people in general, and that lay at the foundation of my shyness.

> Finally we were back on the mountain and lynx said, "This mountain is your fear."
> "I didn't know that what I was doing was killing me," I said to Lynx. "Is it too late now to do anything about it?"
> "If you are willing to face your fear now and experience it completely…," answered Lynx.
> "I'm willing to," I answered frantically.
> "Experience your fear just for the energy that it is."

With this I opened myself up to the experience of the fear that was present in me. I felt the energy of fear begin streaming through my body and my body began writhing on the floor, twisting and stretching, arching itself. Although my eyes were closed it felt as if it might appear to others that I was having a convulsive seizure. This energy of fear flowed and flowed through my body, opening up new avenues in places where for my entire life I has resisted it. I just allowed and my body writhed and writhed. I cried and cried. I don't know how much time had passed, but finally it was over. I was lying still on the floor but in my imagery Lynx and I were sitting calmly by the side of a still lake. I suddenly realized that this lake had been the mountain. It had melted during my convulsions. Each boulder had been some of my frozen fear. I looked at Lynx and thanked him profoundly.

Lynx advised me to face any fear as it arose and to never let it kill me in this way again. I asked lynx if he had a name. He said, "My name is Lynx. I am the link to your wholeness."

"Thank you, thank you," I said.

I allowed myself to return slowly to the room.

There was no hurry. My job was not to take care of the people sitting in the circle but to honor the rhythm of the profound process that I had just been through, and to allow myself all the space and time that I needed. I sometimes think of this as the space surrounding the print on the page in a book. The space honors the print by holding it in a sacred way and in some very fine books there is an excess of space because what is said in print is so valuable. The same esthetic is involved with the time and space that we need to honor concerning our own inner process.

It is not to be hurried. It is not to be judged in terms of the conditioning we have been subjected to about not taking space and time from the group. The most valuable thing in our lives is the inner process which sees to our healing and our coming into maturity.

When I finally opened my eyes I experienced a whole new relationship to the people around me. I was filled with a joyous energy, an energy that I had never felt before. This energy was available as a certain presence for being with people, for connecting with people, whereas my previous propensity for my entire life had been to withdraw.

CHAPTER 12

MY DYING

1990 was the year of my dying. The day my pneumonia was diagnosed my wife and daughter had just left for California to be with their parents and grandparents. This was just after Christmas. I went to bed and began to feel the terror of dying. Great dark spaces appeared in my day and my energy began to wane.

I had scheduled my first seven day workshop with the Big Bear Training Group as the first event in 1990. Fortunately I had also invited Dr. Rene Pelleya to come share his experiences with the group so I called and asked if he would begin the training with them. I felt I might be well enough to arrive midway through the training. I was not. My energy got lower and lower. I was almost too weak to watch television.

I recall watching a football game and as soon as a commercial would appear I would switch to another channel. I suddenly became aware that I was not allowing myself any space. I felt I was trying to jam my time as full of events as possible and I was not allowing any time just to be still. With this realization I relaxed.

My energy never seemed to return fully. I remained short of breath and I tired easily. I changed my schedule to include much less travel even though it meant no longer traveling to the Hartford Family Institute where I had been spending one week a month for the previous four years.

By the time Returning to Earth Institute was held in August I was feeling much better. Once a year, Ann Roberts, Bill Plotkin, Mel Bucholtz and I would take from twelve to fifteen individuals into a wilderness area to enact a two week ceremony of death and rebirth, punctuated by a three day vision quest. The initial week of ceremonial severance is held in a lodge and it generates a lot of energy. Following it we hiked into the Sangre de Cristo Mountains and I felt quite fit. It wasn't until the final mile up the mountain that my backpack began to feel extremely heavy and my chest began to hurt. I kept quiet about it and rested as much as I could. By the second night out people had already dispersed to their individual power spots where they would spend three days fasting and crying for a vision. Only Ann, Bill, Mel and I remained in base camp.

That night lying under my tarp I had difficulty breathing. The air was cold and thin. There was a soft dull pain in my heart. I felt that I would not survive the night and a great terror came over me. I thought I would die from pneumonia or lung failure or hypothermia. I became terrified at the thought of leaving my family and my work, and particularly my daughter who was six years old. I could see people carrying my body down the mountain and I felt sad for my wife and daughter who would be left behind. The terror became intense and I realized that I could not do anything about the dying. If it was my time to die then I would die. I did know that the one thing I could do was to allow myself to feel the terror fully, to go as deeply into it as I could. I realized that the terror had been there all my life. I felt how it had compressed me: my shoulders, my back, my breathing. I began to see that the terror was also a terror of my father, that I had been terrified of my father almost all my life, feeling how desperately I wanted him to love me, how I loved him, how I hated him.

I saw a scene when I was seven years old. I was talking to my mother. She was asking me about my father and I told her that I was afraid of him but I asked her to promise not to tell him. She promised.

That same night I was lying in my bed and I could hear my parents talking. She was telling him that I was afraid of him and he was scornful. I was startled to hear her do this. I felt I could no longer trust her. The one person to whom I could still express myself freely was now gone and from then on I clammed up, became relatively mute and depressed. That was also when I began to love people in secret.

I saw that my terror of death was also a terror of life, was also the terror that I projected out onto the wilderness and the unknown. The greatest terror, it felt like, was of my power, and of the fact that I may misuse it as my father had. Still, the terror and death were intricately interwoven. I slept only a few fitful hours during the night.

The next morning I still had a shortness of breath and my midsection was quivering. I could not find a spot to be that was comfortably warm. Ann and Mel were off hiking. I went to Bill and told him about the night and that I had some concern about dying. He listened attentively as I described my thoughts and feelings. He told me that although the possibility that there may be some heart problems existed, the symptoms sounded very much like those resulting from intense fear. He offered to guide me while I consulted with my animals about it.

As I called out for any animal that needed to visit with me I was surprised to see Bear approach, slinking along like a raccoon.

Bear was the first heart animal I ever met and I had not seen him in many years. I greeted him and he just opened his arms and held me, stroking my back while I cried. I felt overwhelmed at my father's cruelty and I grieved deeply over the lack of a relationship with him. I told Bear that I was also sorry that my own son had died. Bear replied that I wasn't ready to have a son until I got through what I was going through now.

I told Bear that my heart hurt and he said just to let it break. I cried and cried, deeply, wrenchingly. When it abated Bear said that I would just have to find a new heart. When I asked him where he just scratched his head in puzzlement, so we went to visit Eagle.

Eagle was flying around in circles, high in the air. I asked him if he knew what had been going on and he said that he had been watching it all my life. I asked him if we could go find my new heart and he replied that he needed to take me to see something first.

Eagle picked me up and flew me to a scene in my father's boyhood. I could see a very small adobe house below, far out in the country. It was a scene of abject poverty. Eagle showed me that my father was the oldest of thirteen children and his mother's favorite. His father was much older than his mother.

As each of the new children was born my father was jealous of it. Eagle also showed me a scene of my grandfather beating my father with a stick, violently. Eagle said that he wanted me to know where my father's cruelty had originated.

Eagle, Bear and I then went to meet Whale at the edge of the sea. Whale had been my original belly animal and he said that he would take us to my new heart. He opened his mouth and we all went in. I thought that he was going to take us to a distant land but he headed straight for the ocean bottom. All of my original animals were there waiting: Rabbit, Stag, and White Horse. I was delighted to see them and deeply moved by the reunion.

Whale showed me a large treasure chest and asked me to open it. Inside was a large heart, decorated around the edges in a way that I couldn't see clearly. As Bear helped me put the new heart in my chest the other animals cheered. I asked Whale how I could repay him and his answer was to show people my heart. I cried.

All the animals came along as Whale took us to a sandy beach. Here we formed a circle around a fire and the animals said we would now have to spend some time contemplating my new heart. I thanked the animals for being there for me and for the experience they had just guided me through.

I opened my eyes and thanked Bill. The pain had abated significantly following this journey but there was still some pain in my heart. So I hiked down the mountain, got in my car, and drove to a nearby community. There was no doctor in this community but there was a small medical trailer. I went in and told them that I wanted to have my heart checked as there was some pain in it. They listened to my heart and did an EKG and then told me that they could find nothing wrong with my heart so they were sending for an ambulance that would drive me to the emergency room at Taos hospital. I was stunned at this and inquired: you mean because you can find nothing wrong with my heart you are sending me to the emergency room of a hospital? Yes, they replied, there may be something we are missing.

I found this incredulous and told them that I would drive there myself, since I had my own car. They refused and insisted on calling an ambulance. I was equally insistent and told them that I would not go in an ambulance. Finally, after much stressful negotiation that itself could have brought on a heart attack they insisted that I sign a release absolving them of any responsibility, which I did. This entire event was so funny and at the same time so tragic. I felt the organization treating me as one of its prisoners. I got in my car and drove to the Pueblo Cafe, ordered enchiladas which I ate with gusto and drove back to the foot of the mountain, climbed it and rejoined the vision quest.

CHAPTER 13

BEING THE DRUM

At a training in Germany, Gerhardt, one of the students who is also a drum maker, has brought his personal drum with him. It is a beautiful drum covered with the skin of a gemse, a chamois goat, with a stripe down the center.

During the training I find myself in a small group with Gerhardt. As I myself relax for my own journey, I call out within myself for an animal guide. My guide is immediately there. It is a chamois goat similar to the one whose skin covers Gerhardt's drum, with a stripe down the back.

I ask the goat what needs to happen here and it asks me to beat it on the back with two drum sticks. I am very hesitant about beating it. When I finally do the sound is beautiful but it brings back many memories of the times my father beat me as a little boy.

The goat says, "Look, I gave up my life to make this beautiful sound. What did you give up?"

The goat tells me again to beat it on the back. I again take the drumsticks and beat... I feel my hesitation... it feels like doing to it what my father did to me and I realize how I have rejected that... as I beat it an energy begins to run through my arms. I have never allowed this energy. It also feels like the energy that came out in the crafts that I did as a boy.

The chamois goat asks if I know that I have a stripe down my back the way it does. It asks if it can beat me. I say yes. It takes the drumsticks and beats me on my back and it sounds like the sixty years of my life and it's the sound that touches many people. I see the beatings my father gave me resounding throughout sixty years and ending in the work that I do with the animals. The sounds of those beatings have been transformed and have now become beautiful sounds, like the drum. The energy of the beatings seeking their own transformation, like the drum, when you beat it, teaching other people. Somehow the whole world makes sense when understood like that, injuries being opportunities for transformation.

It brings me to a place where I realize I must accept all these beatings and I'm aware that I have always tried to exclude them from my life. I have to honor them and recognize that they are an essential part of my path. It seems like it probably really did hurt my father more than it hurt me, because he lost a son he could have had. The feeling is very strange. It's accepting something I never accepted. Since I never accepted it, I never accepted my life as it is.

The goat is still beating but it's a much slower rhythm now, very deep, African, very ancient. What I'm hearing is a really old, old understanding of our injuries transforming into something beautiful. At first he was beating me on my tail and now he's beating me on my shoulders and neck. It doesn't hurt.

It is like an energy. It feels like a place in my body that I constricted. The beating of the chamois goat is opening that up again. As the chamois goat is beating on my back something is changing in my spine.

I see a key and I am going into a keyhole now. I say hello and ask if it has something to tell me but it doesn't answer. It's in my back. I find myself wearing a pair of boots made of chamois leather and I ask the chamois goat if anything in particular needs to happen and it says yes. It's jumping now. Someone is bringing me something to eat, like stew. I can't see who it is. I don't know what's happening now.

Chamois goat says, "Let's take your skin off and make a drum." I see my skin now over a drum. It's fine, not heavy and thick like the mountain goats skin.

Chamois goat tells me it needs my heart. I offer my heart and it takes it and places it right into the center of the drum. As my heart beats the drum beats. It feels good.

Now there's something happening with the skin of my body. I'm seeing a road I never saw before. This road is also a dishpan full of dishes and some bread.

Now mountain goat is standing on top of the mountain. From there we can see everything. I have two eyes: one sees through imagery and feeling and the other through thinking and sensing. But they're both seeing as one.

I suddenly understand that when I was beaten by my father my spine contracted. Being beaten by the mountain goat has opened it up again, it is returning to its original flexibility. As I return slowly to the room where I am lying on the floor I feel my skin resonating, vibrating. I feel my arms vibrating also. I feel wonderful.

CHAPTER 14

DADDY, COME HOME

In the advanced portion of the trainings that I have developed we undergo some exercises that are intended to deepen and broaden the students intuitive knowing. During the first year of training the student has been constantly focused on using their imagery to look within themselves, primarily at the energies in their own chakras. But in the second year they begin to use their imagery to look at the energies emanating from another person's chakras.

Two precautions are always in order. The first precaution is that some of their own energy may be obscuring the energy they see emanating from the other person, so that what they see may have more to do with them than with the other person. They should always recognize that at least some of what they are seeing may come from their own inner dynamics. The second precaution is that they are never to look into the other person's chakras without the other's permission.

Some other aspects of this exercise are that the person reading the chakra energy is not to judge, not to evaluate what they see in terms of its meaning, but to recognize that what they see may be only one facet of a much deeper ongoing process. Room must always be allowed for the mystery of the other person's process; not everything can be known and nailed down within our ability to conceptualize. Also, they are never to impose what they see on the other person but always to recognize it as an aspect of their own seeing. This helps one return to a natural respect for one's own perception and to recognize that not all of one's experiences can be consensually validated. Consensual validation is not the ultimate determiner of value.

The first part of the exercise is focussed on the reading. Hedwig is my guide. She begins by asking if I will give her my permission to use her imagery for looking at the energy in my chakras. I do. The following is what she sees:

In your forehead I see a diamond, sparkling, with one side longer than the others. It sparkles in red, green and blue. There is a light fog around it, not nearly as heavy as it has been, like the day following a rain.

In your heart I see a large bear, somewhat aggressive, who has a black spot on his fur that needs to be dealt with. He lies in a meadow, in the flowers, eating honey.

In your solar plexus I see a white sheet with something colorful behind it.

In your belly is a snake. It is black and green and sparkles in the sunlight. It sits in a kind of desert with some flowers around. It shows the way to the water. It looks like the river at River Spirit. It goes to the bank of the river and says, "That's where I'm at home."

In your grounding is a flame that just has a slight glow to it.

In your throat chakra I see your throat and in it area number of animals who say it needs to be widened, and they are trying to stretch it.

In your eighth chakra there is a Virgin, a beautiful woman who is bright. She is enswathed in something like a rope of light. She emerges from it like she is being born. She says she is your connection to the Universe and she has been waiting for a long time to be born. She's very sensitive right now. It can happen that she will hide again. You should care for her but you also cannot hold her in that place. Now she's going back into your body, she's half in and half out. There's a very strong pull to the inside and she's going back inside now. At the appropriate time she will appear again. Light is still shining in that place.

Following the reading the exercise shifts. The person whose chakras have just been read (in this particular case, me) is now prompted by the reader to ask within themselves if there is anything in the reading that should be journeyed into further. This journey, if it is undertaken, usually casts some light on the validity of what the reader has just seen. They may also see that what may have seemed obscure may actually have some potent depth, and recognize that they are seeing an aspect but not the total dynamic of the person's inner process. And it also helps both parties recognize that anything at all can be the doorway to a journey.

When I ask inside if there are any of these elements that I should journey with I am taken immediately to my throat. It is a vertical mine shaft and little animals are suspended by ropes. They all have little picks and buckets and are trying to open up the mine shaft.

They ask me to come help them. I ask if I should help them from where I'm lying on the mat or if I should join them there. They say, "Both!" I see myself being lowered in a bucket on a rope. I have a miner's hat on and a pick in my hands. I ask what I should do and they say that I should play music to them. I'm surprised at this request because I thought they would ask me to excavate with them. I begin to play music that has a very particular beat to it, like the cadence of a poem. They immediately become coordinated and as they strike simultaneously at the mine wall I see it expanding. The music is reminiscent of an old folksong. I hear a trumpet playing somewhere in the distance and the beat is similar to the music I'm playing.

Now all the animals are holding a blanket under me and tossing me in the air, as if I were on a trampoline. They are all coordinated. It feels good. I suddenly hear a voice say, "Daddy, Daddy... come home...come home." I don't know who it is. My daughter, Nikaya? My own voice as a child? I follow the voice. What does it mean to come home? I see my current home, River Spirit, and the voice is coming from there, but I don't see anyone. The place itself is calling me. I ask if I should go there really, and a voice says, "Yes." I begin thinking of catching a standby flight, but Nikaya is here in Germany with me, and I have the training to conduct. How could I go?

Now I see my childhood home. I see my mother and two children, me and my older sister, Juliet. We are all outside in the adobe garage whose construction has been underway for years. It still has no roof on it and the New Mexico sun is beating down on us. My mother is washing clothes in a washer that has a gasoline motor.

Suddenly we see *El Mal Hijo* coming down the highway on his little cart. This was a man who lived in Los Lentes. He had no legs and made his way around on a small hand built cart with low wheels. He would propel himself along by two wooden blocks that he held in his hands. We never knew his real name. The story was that as a young man he had kicked his mother and his legs had fallen off. This is how he had acquired the name *El Mal Hijo* (The Bad Son). I once heard my mother ask my grandmother Martina if this story were true and she said it was not.

My mother was terrified of this man. We watched as he made his way along the highway that ran in front of our house, highway 85, and then he suddenly turned and began to make his way down our driveway. My mother gathered me and my sisters up and ran inside, locked the door, and we hid, peeking out the window. *El Mal Hijo* could not make it up the steps and he yelled something in Spanish from where he was. My mother's terror was tangible. Eventually, he turned around and made his way back up the rather steep and long driveway. We all gave a sigh of relief and then my mother said wistfully, "Maybe he only wanted a drink of water."

I become aware of how frightened my mother was when she was alone with us, when Daddy was at work. He gave her a sense of security. I've never seen this part of him, this security. In one way I am calling him for my mother's sake, so that she can feel safe. I was really afraid for her. She couldn't protect us. I realize how much a part of her security he was. She really relied on him in order to feel safe.

I didn't feel safe when he was home, he punished me so much. I see the kind of bind I was caught in, a strange kind of bind to be in. I see what a conflict I was in: if I called him in order for my mother to be safe, then I wasn't safe. Yet when my mother was afraid I felt her fear. There was no way out.

The conflict has been there all my life: wanting to call him (for her sake) and not call him at the same time. Wanting to speak and to not speak at the same time. My mother encouraged me to speak and my father to keep quiet. It's very old and very deep. My voice has been divided. I feel it throughout my entire body. Acting and not acting at the same time, in order to be safe. I feel how my entire face closed down in that conflict, my lips, my jaw, my gums, my neck, my ears.

Suddenly I'm back in my bucket. All the animals are around me cheering.

I find myself now at my root chakra. A fire is there and a bellows. I am working the bellows in order to increase the fire. The heat of the fire builds and travels up through my body until it emerges through my mouth. My mouth is getting the energy from that fire.

I am a blacksmith, heating the metal and pounding it. Fathers come by with their sons and tell the sons what I am doing, even though I myself don't know. They don't just let the kids have the experience, but they have to explain it to them. The kid only wanted to watch and enjoy and have his own questions. I remember asking my own father questions and he either had no reply or else he made fun of my questions. I stopped asking him questions. The questions stayed in me, in their own fire. I am seeing that fire. It was so vital that it continued to burn. I feel how my body formed itself around those questions, to protect them, so that the fire would not go out. Those questions were essential to my growth, to my development, to my path, to my quest. The fire says to me, "I never go out."

So I am appreciating my father. Because he wouldn't answer my questions on the outside they kept on burning on the inside. They set the course for my path. My path could not have happened without them.

So I speak to my father and tell him how essential he was for my path. I honor him and realize that the relationship we had was vital even if it was not what I wanted at that time.

"Daddy, the way you were with me has been vital to my journey!" I see the significance to my path. Every aspect is important. I never thought of this possibility. It hurts when I say it.

I hear again, "Daddy, Daddy. Come home, come home." And I hear it now in a totally different way. Like I really am calling my father back home. It's a part of me that I always rejected. The black spot on the bear was my relationship with my father and my heart had never honored that.

I see that the vertical mine shaft is now completely open and it opens directly into my heart. I hear "Daddy, Daddy! You've come home!" Now I feel completely safe. My anger toward my father is finally finished. I could not have walked my path without him. He was vital to it. Something very old has healed in me. I have come home. My father has come home.

CHAPTER 15

THE WILD BOY
& THE TAMED

One of the primary consequences of being animals that speak is that we become locked into a division. We take these divisions to be aspects of reality. We divide the flow of time into day and night and feel that such a division is natural. But in doing so we lose all the subtle gradations. We become blind to the sudden intensification of darkness that occurs just before the first light of dawn. We lose the fine shifts and gradations as light skips from darkness into sunlight, and the mysterious experience of the crack between the worlds, the soft layers of dusk.

We see ourselves as being alive and fearing death rather than knowing the continuity between them. We see the world as good and bad, blind to the judgments we make which fix the world in that way.We see students as dumb or smart and lose the specific quality of the unique path that each being has on this earth. In the United States we become caught in the division between young and old, trapped in a valuing activity of our own making. Perhaps one of the aspects of our own aliveness that we are most blind to is the division between the wild and the tame.

I was at a training in Pennsylvania. I felt a pain in the upper left part of my heart. The pain had been brought on by an intense projection onto me of some anger that really belonged to an ex-husband who I resembled. The woman knew she was projecting and voiced it. I also knew she was projecting, but the pain was there, nonetheless.

"We are caught in an energy here in which we are both participating," I said to her, "and I need to journey to see my own part in it."

I asked Tony, the only other man in the group, to guide me. He agreed. He helped me relax and asked me to call out for a guide who knew what needed to happen.

I call out for a guide and I see a man climbing a ladder out of what looks like a coal cellar. He is a cartoon character that I recognize out of The New Yorker magazine, he is mostly head and nose. The opening from which he emerges is also an opening into my heart where the pain is located.

I ask him, "What needs to happen here?", and he invites me to follow him down the ladder. The opening is dark and dusty and I climb in after him. It feels like the cellar of this house in the mountains where we are holding the training and also like the cellar in the house where I grew up in New Mexico. It is dark and strangely cold. We continue climbing down and down. I didn't realize the cellar was that deep. I know my guide is ahead of me (although I can't see him because we are both climbing down feet first the way one climbs down a ladder), but I don't know what's beyond that. I'm amazed at how steady the ladder is, but as I say this the ladder begins to jiggle. It feels like someone is standing at the bottom shaking it. As we go deeper the pain in my heart becomes more intense, particularly in the left side of my heart.

Tony, who is guiding this session, invites me to ask if there is anything my guide can tell me about this pain. I ask him and he replies, "Oh, da pain, Mon, dot pain. Da pain been wid you long, long time!" I am surprised and amused by his Jamaican accent, and I ask how long the pain has been with me. As I ask the question I realize it has been there since I was a little boy, and that it has something to do with that cellar. I see a memory of me as a child, in that cellar with my father. We are both standing talking and he feels lustful toward me. He suddenly picks me up and spanks me. I realize for the first time that there is a sexual aspect to all of the punishment that I received from him. I ask my guide what it is I am supposed to see in this situation and he replies, "Just dot, Mon." I then ask where we are going. "Oh, deeper dan dot," he replies. We have reached the floor of the basement but the ladder continues down a smaller opening, into what seems like a basement to the basement. As we enter this new opening another memory appears.

I was about two or three years old. I deeply loved and honored my father. I would have done anything at all for him but there was nothing I did that pleased him. I remember a time when he spanked me. I was angry and ran outside and wrote on the side of a metal bin, "I do not like Daddy." Sometime later he returned from Albuquerque and brought me a hat just like his. I was so happy at this gift, but as he handed it to me he said, "Maybe now you won't write those bad things about me any more." I felt like I had been stabbed and came to hate that hat. Every pathway to loving him was blocked. Every attempt to identify with him was stifled.

I ask my guide, "Are we dere yet, Mon?" , imitating his accent, "Oh, no, my friend," he answers, "we're not quite there yet." I am surprised at this switch in his accent and I say to him, "You won't let me identify with you, will you?" He answers, "Oh, no, Mon."

The opening through which we are climbing down is getting narrower. I remember as a child yearning for someone that I could be like, someone I could identify with, someone I admired and could model myself after, and there was no one. I tell my guide about the yearning and he answers, "I know dot, Mon. Keep climbing. We going beyond dot."

I suddenly understand that my father's punishment of my attempted identification with him was a gift. The fact that I could not model my behavior after him, doing the things that he did, forced me to search for myself. Who was I? What did I like? What did I think? What was of importance to me? And that search had carried me deep into myself and brought me to the path that I was currently walking.

Now the passageway is very narrow and square. I just fit through the opening. I remember having dreams as a child of crawling through a tunnel and the terror of getting stuck in it. But that was head first, this time we are going in feet first. I tell my guide about these memories and he replies, "Don't worry about dot, Mon. We not going to get stuck, we going to get FREE!"

I feel a real trust in this guide, a real trust. I tell him that and he answers that having a trust in him is having a trust in myself. I am aware I have never gone this deep into my heart before. As we continue climbing down I tell him that my intentions are good, and that if they're not I'm willing to look at that.

We have come to the bottom. It is a deep, deep cave lined with crystals. I think to myself, "Wow, we are in the crystal cave!" There is a soft brightness to it. My guide says, "We at rock bottom here, Mon." I ask my guide where we are, and he answers, "Dis is de place of you frozen tears, Mon, frozen tears." I realize that this is a cold and frozen place in my heart. I ask my guide how this happened. He shows me myself as a young child: wild, active, curious, exploring, adventuresome, willing to risk. I loved this dimension of myself, this true aliveness. It thrilled me. My guide shows me getting punishment after punishment, rejection after rejection, whenever this dimension of myself was active. I freeze that part of myself little by little until I am square, acceptable, predictable, lifeless, lonely, without any juice of my own. Until I am completely obedient. By then my focus is completely on my parents: what is acceptable to them, what kind of punishment would be coming from them, until I am completely vigilant and obedient!

I hated myself! I hated the little obedient kid I had become! Totally dependent! No juice at all! Totally looking outside! I hated that little kid who was good! I see him above on the surface of the earth and I tell him how much I hated him and he replies sadly, "Everybody hated me." It feels like I turned all my anger onto him, so that any anger that came from anyone else fit right in the alignment was already in place.

I tell my guide how much I hated that boy. My guide says, "Hey, Mon, wid out him you would never have made it! You would have been beaten to death!" In myself I feel he is right, and I say, "Maybe it would have been better that way!" My guide replies emphatically, "No, Mon! You had things to do!" I ask my guide what I should do with the wild boy who is frozen in tears.

"Ask him to rejoin you."

I feel such an extreme division. This is the most extreme polarity I have ever encountered. I place my left arm around the good, obedient, almost lifeless boy, the boy who takes his cues almost completely from people in the external world. My right arm is around the wild boy. He is deeply bitter and vicious, angry. His life is still very frozen but it is his aliveness. I tell them "I don't know how we're going to do it but I need to love you both."

The boy on the left is soft and smooth, the one on the right is rigid and hard, with sharp spikes. I suddenly become aware that the one place they met was in my art! In the crafts I practiced as a child. The aliveness and originality of the wild boy joined forces with the control and awareness of the obedient boy at this place and they produced some beautiful things: a wallet that I gave to my father, a belt for my mother, my crafts were usually given as gifts. This was the only way I could show who I am!

I tell them, "I know that for very long you have both been told who and what you are. I'm willing to listen to you, to hear who you are directly from you. If we need to drop everything else and do art together we'll do art."

I see myself at River Spirit with them both. We are doing the healing we need to do between us by building with adobes. I ask them what they need from me. The boy on my right is content to have my arm around him. The boy on the left says he wants to beloved. The boy on the right says that's all he wanted, too. I suddenly become aware of how deeply I rejected them both. I am aware I have not identified with either of them and that this has left me very empty. I acknowledge this to them and tell them that without them I am nothing. They are vital, essential to my being. The ice begins to melt.

I also begin to recognize that whereas the wild boy embodies spontaneity and deep aliveness the tame boy has developed the capacity to know what others are going to ask him or tell him, a deeply intuitive sense. And he also has the quality of control and precision in his actions. I ask my guide if anything more needs to happen.

He informs me that we need to stay in both the deepest place in my heart and at River Spirit. We need to maintain a full open passageway between these two places and between both of these boys. I feel a vital energy connection up my arms. They are still separate energies and maybe they always will be. I need to stay fully in touch and honor them both.

I say to my guide, "Anything else need to hoppen here, Mon?" He replies, "Oh, no. We've taken care of things quite well."

I realize that if I had identified with my father I would never have met these energies, these two boys. I would have been lost in their division. In their separation they guarded my wholeness!

I thank my guide and he bows in gassho. I bow as well. I thank the two boys and myself for enduring. I thank the woman who through her projection was the doorway for this healing experience. I thank Tony, my external guide, and everyone around.

HONORING THE WILD CHILD

After returning to the windows of sensing and thinking I realized that although this is my story it is also the story of everyone who belongs to our Western culture. The Wild Child is essential to our aliveness and to our wholeness. The next day I feel myself solid and whole as never before.

Since this journey, and as my healing continues, I have come to see just how thoroughly we tame our children. And just how we fear their wildness! We teach them to be obedient even in rejection of their own knowing. We train them to be obedient to language, to respond to language with language of their own, and in this way further divorce them from their other ways of knowing. We have set up school as a place of obedience training, not a place where they discover their own qualities, not a place for exploration of their boundaries. Not a place where they could safely venture into the unknown of who they are. We train them as if they were soldiers. We divorce them from their own living souls. We interrupt their own attention with a shrill bell, we dictate to them the time and the topic of their interest, we label them as having attention deficit disorders if they fail to attend to the things we deem important and force them away from the natural living flow of their own awareness.

When we train an animal we mark its progress by whether or not it will respond to our direction rather than its own; when it responds to our words then it is trained. We deem it tame when it does not attack us but does our bidding, even if by rights it should attack us for what we have done to it. And we treat our children no differently: we expect them to pay attention when we say something to them rather than ourselves becoming aware of the places where their attention goes naturally. We expect them to say Yes, Sir and No, Ma'am like robots, we expect them to respond like servants when we issue orders. How often are we willing to accompany them in some activity as friends, as companions?

The child's wildness is nothing to be feared. It is at the heart of his creativity and aliveness. It is a thing to be feasted upon and harvested, it is the fruit of his being, it is at the core of his aliveness. Since we have come to fear our own aliveness, our own wildness, our own inner wilderness, we fear that of others. And yet we have created, especially in America, one of the most feared cultures anywhere: where we lock our doors and live in gated communities, where we fear wilderness and naturalness, and feel safe only when animals are caged in zoos and criminals are behind bars. We do that which is politically correct rather than relishing the original knowing of our inherent wildness. It is also in our wildness that our knowing how to be with one another in a deeply human way resides.

CHAPTER 16

A NEW ENERGY LEVEL

Our injuries freeze us in particular behaviors. Although our responses to injury may prove to have value at the time of their onset, they do become frozen and so repeat themselves. Thus they come to be detrimental because they restrict our flexibility and detract from our full potential. In the following journey I deal with an injury that originated not in an intense trauma but in the repeated patterns of my own parents in their dealings with me.

Lying on the floor, relaxed, I call out within myself and ask if there is an animal or a guide that can come to me for this journey. My guide arrives immediately and it is Bugs Bunny. He is snappy and quick, tells me to follow him and he hurries along at a rapid pace. As I follow I become aware that my right arm and side feel very heavy, leaden, dead. As I hurry behind Bugs, I feel I am just dragging them along, or, that my right side is passively resisting the new pace.

I remember my mother trying to get me to do things for her, treating me like a servant, and me resisting in this same manner, doing whatever it was but very slowly so that my pace was frustrating to her. I realize that my right side has been doing this ever since then, opposing whatever I was ordered to do, just automatically opposing. I realize that my right side is covered with armor from the middle ages. Furthermore it is make our of lead! I shuck off the lead armor that covers my right side.

Then Bugs and I are in a field. We scurry over a fence into the next field where there is a large bull. We scurry and dance around the bull so fast that he doesn't know which way to turn. Then we form a spiral, or a whirlwind, and go around and around the bull. The whirlwind becomes narrower and begins to penetrate the bull's solar plexus. I feel at the same time like my own energy is shifting. I realize I have always thought of stillness as being somewhat leaden, torpor-like, but here I see that there is a new possibility for stillness: energized and sparkling, still but not dull. I feel my body sparkling at this new energy level.

I then become aware of a pain that has been in my right shoulder for almost twenty years. Bugs begins to dive into my shoulder and soon looks like a mechanic under a car. He says he needs to replace the generator. He disconnects some wires and then has difficulty disconnecting them at the other end. Eventually he has to follow the wire to its place of insertion, which feels like my right elbow. As he disconnects it my arm twists and I feel the pain. He takes out the old generator and installs a newer model, more compact. As he hooks it up my arm again twists and the pain leaves.

I then ask Bugs what needs to happen now and he says we need to clean up the mess. He begins putting tools away. I realize it is like my father's garage, and I hear his voice saying, "If you use a tool put it back where it belongs!", which I seldom did. Bugs makes everything very orderly and says to me: If you put it back where it belongs, then you'll know where it is when you need it again. I feel the spaciousness and comfort of the garage organized and I see my own disorganized desk, and realize that my disorganization is my way of opposing my father, just as my leaden slowness was my way of opposing my mother. Hopefully both of those are gone now.

I return feeling a renewed energy and an easy sparkling quality with the people in the training. That evening we sit very comfortably around the fire and talk easily, something that has seldom been easy for me.

CHAPTER 17

THE EXECUTIONER

One of the curious aspects of being human is our tendency toward psychological projection. Simply put, psychological projection involves experiencing others as doing something that we ourselves are in fact doing blindly. The following journey wakes me up to the fact that the way in which I feel judged by others is actually the result of my own judging of them. The uncanny ability of deep imagery to use a completely illogical situation as a powerful instructional experience is also fascinating.

I am laying on a mat and my human guide sits at my side. I must be very ready for this journey because there is not even time for a relaxation. As soon as I close my eyes I see a powerfully built man with a black hood over his head. Holes are cut for his eyes although I can't see his eyes. He is holding an executioner's broad axe. It is finely honed. I am next to him with my head on a block of wood. He swings his axe and cuts my head off. It rolls into the sand and dust.

I then ask him what more needs to happen and he invites me to come with him. We sit at an outdoor cafe table and order some food. I am sitting on a chair to his right but my head is disconnected from my body and is floating above and forward. The food arrives and he eats with gusto. I eat also but the food falls out of my severed throat onto the ground.

I understand that my head is disconnected from my body, and I see how full of worry and doubt and thoughts my head is. I see myself as a child and how powerless I felt when my father and mother both had thoughts about me. I knew that their thoughts and their collusion were not me but I felt powerless, captured by their thoughts and contained by them. I see a meeting that I am supposed to be attending, and how I fear that decisions will be made which will then restrict or contain me in some way.

I become aware of how I feel locked into other people's judgements of me, as if by a magnet. I see that I give my energy to their judgments and then feel bound by them, as if I am captured in some way, but I realize how I participate in it. I see myself as a child. Whenever my father was around I was fully attentive to his judgments of me, and of protecting myself from them. I see how I have perpetuated this orientation, of being so fully focused on the judgements of others and of the need to protect myself from them.

The executioner says: You want to control other people's judgements of you!

I see myself holding a heavy broadsword. My arms are tired. I have been judging others with one edge of this blade and protecting myself from their judgement with the other. I have been judging them in the same way I myself have felt judged.

I see that I am wary of being captured and held by the judgements of others, and executioner asks me who I am. As I look I can only see the fluidity of my experiences of the moment, and I tell him I don't know. I see how others also don't really know who they are, or else they mistake themselves for a concept. I see that I am just a fluid luminosity.

Executioner tells me that I must let that luminosity fill each role that I must play. I see how I have been avoiding roles, exerting all my energy not to enter into any role. Executioner shows me that roles are the fabric of society, and that the secret is not to avoid roles but also not to get stuck in them, to put them on and take them off depending on the circumstances and the situation, and to let my luminosity shine forth from within each role.

I see my head returning to my neck and body.

Executioner comes around behind me and begins to stitch my head and body together with a small needle and white thread. He tells me that this is also a sword, but this is the sword of connection rather than of separation, and that I must learn to wield that sword as well.

CHAPTER 18

THE BANDIT SONG

The experience of being fully at home in the natural juiciness of who we are, being alive and relishing the fact without an agenda, is one of the delicious aspects of our being. A kind of sassiness, loving being alive, was hidden and lacking in me for too long. In the following journey I am reintroduced to this quality.

Lying on the mat I call out for my guide and immediately I see a donkey. It is sweet-looking, grey with a white face. It is a Mexican burro, with sad, soft eyes. I see that it is being led by someone, it has a large load on its back.

I ask the man who is leading the burro what is happening. I have the thought that he is Juan Valdez and that we are on a coffee plantation, but as he turns to me I see the fullness of his Mexican face, and his energy is just bursting forth, full, very full. He is wearing banderillas and draws his pistol, points it at me, and tells me to walk ahead of him. So the three of us continue on into the mountains, me in the lead with the pistol at my back, then the Mexican, and then the burro whose reins he holds.

We arrive at a cave and enter into it. Deep inside I see a fire burning. As we reach the fire I see that there is a large group of Mexican bandidos (bandits) standing around it. They greet me and make jokes, asking me, *Hey, Gringo, para que has venido aqa?* (Why have you come here?), and similar things, joking and jesting. They are full of laughter. The fullness of the Mexican masculine brotherhood is in them.

A memory comes to me of a journey I took years ago. I had asked for a guide to take me to the origin of the cruelty in my father's culture. I wanted to go there to do whatever I could to bring it to an end, so that it would not be perpetuated any longer. I was led back to the earliest times of humanity, to a group of men deep in a cave around a fire. There I was shown that there had been a time during the ice age when the small tribe that eventually became my father's culture had been on the edge of extinction. The people were starving. If there was any game around the children had to be perfectly still and not make a sound because the tribe could not afford to let the game escape. The survival of the tribe was at stake. Thus children were taught not to move or speak until a grown-up had told them it was okay. The situation was so drastic and survival was so in question for such a long time that this orientation became frozen into the culture even once the circumstances had changed.

The thought comes to me that the place the bandido and his burro have brought me to now, perhaps this is the polarity of the cruelty: the richness, fullness of feeling, comradeship. Then one of the bandidos takes a guitar and begins to sing. It is a sad song, but it is not only sad, it is quite emotionally complex. I begin to realize that I have been trying to sort out my feelings since I arrived here and to come to what I really feel, but that I have actually been narrowing my feelings, and trying to distill them rather than just allowing them to be in their natural fullness and complexity. I have been trying to figure out what I feel rather than just feeling everything I feel whether I am able to articulate it or not.

I then begin to remember how dearly I loved Mexican songs as a boy, and how I learned the words to many of them, and how I loved the musical aspect of Mexican culture. I then sing a song for these men. They listen attentively and respectfully. Then they express their appreciation for my having sung it. I begin to realize that I have always hidden my love for Mexican music, that I have sung to myself but not when others were around. I then sing *La Feria de las Flores, "Me gustacantarle al viento porque vuelan mis cantares, y dicen lo que yo siento, por toditos los lugares."* (The Festival of the Flowers: I like to sing to the wind because my songs then fly and say what I am feeling in all directions). I realize that the song is really about me, about how I need to sing, to the wind, not to anyone, but just because I love and feel.

The burro begins to grow and is transformed into a beautiful horse. We all head out of the cave and stand around a fire out in the open. It is dusk. The bandidos give me two banderillas which cross over my heart and they put me on the horse. They acknowledge me as one of them and I am deeply moved. I realize I have returned to a part of my culture that I have only owned secretly. One where songs are sung feelingly, where feelings are expressed without concern for results, where there is a blossoming of aliveness, comradeship, masculine energy. I realize my mother was always afraid of this aspect of me, the full masculine expressiveness, and that my father punished me whenever I became expressive, but I have clung to this in secret, the fullness of the masculine. I realize I must return to Mexico and really love there that which I love.

I leave the group of men and head out across the desert now, riding my horse and singing. We travel throughout the night, through a beautiful, unbelievably starry sky, and at dawn we cross the border into the United States. The sky is open, a beautiful clear day is dawning. I arrive at my home in New Mexico on the Rio Grande, a place named River Spirit, and see myself singing and working. Not singing to anyone but just because the song is there. The spirit of the horse, very large, is there at River Spirit also.

CHAPTER 19

THE GAP

I am at a training in New York and we have split up into groups of two. I go to the bathroom just before I am to journey. In this bathroom there is a poster of a baby, a boy, looking at his mother's teat with great fascination, but there is also something wistful and longing in his gaze.

I lie down on the bed and Ellen guides me through a beautiful relaxation. I call out within myself inviting an animal to come forth and am startled at who it is that appears: the boy from the poster! I greet him and ask him what needs to happen here. He plunges me immediately into a series of early experiences and realizations.

I am an infant and have just been weaned, too early. I feel desperate: how do I get back to that warm and nurturing breast that is so comforting? I experience a tremendous hunger, but it is more than a hunger for food; my entire being hungers for the experience of being held, hungers for the smell and the warmth of the breast, of the deeply satisfying presence of mother, of clinging to the teat through my own actions, of drawing in the warm, sweet milk that fills my being. What must I do to bring back that vital link into my life? I am desperate!

Then suddenly I am four years old. We are in the living room of our three-room adobe house. My mother is sitting in the rocking chair next to the coal heater. I ask her if I can sit in her lap but she is very pregnant. She asks my father if he can do something with me, implying that I could sit on his lap. In a gruff voice he says to me, "You're too old to be sitting in someone's lap anymore! You're a grown boy. Go and do something else."

I feel a pain in my heart at this rejection and the excruciating loss of vital connection. I see that I subsequently develop a callus around this event. I harden and become insensitive. I deny my need for that connection. I deny that I need anything. So I become rejecting, rejecting of my own needs, of my need to be connected in a nurturing way. And I see that this old reaction is still present in my current life. It traps me in a narrow place in my relationships with women: needing but not able to get too close for fear of losing myself, of merging with them, and then not being able to separate myself.

I am shown that there is a gap in my development. My father should have been able to help me through this gap but he couldn't because he also had such a gap. He himself was treated in such a way when he was young, needing his mother and not being allowed that connection. For me the gap involves a panic at the possible loss of a nurturing connection and then my own rejection of my needs and of the possibility of being connected.

As I watch, the boy, my guide, breaches the gap by saying to his mother: "I know I can no longer sit in your lap but I miss the closeness we had. Is there some way we could still stay in contact?" She hears him, puts her arm around him and tells him a story. It is good and warm, and father is also soothed by the story. So from the brittleness of that gap I see the possibility of communicating my needs and negotiating them, so that some flexibility develops.

I see Rosemary, the first girl I dated and fell in love with when I was a teenager. I was madly in love with her, she was the first girl I had ever kissed. Suddenly she stopped seeing me with no explanation. I was distraught, heartbroken, confused, and didn't know what to think. At the time I felt that her rejection of me was somehow my fault, but I know now that she had started dating someone else. I realize that I have usually felt that being rejected is somehow my fault rather than being able to see the larger picture.

My guide begins to grow, transforming into a firm but warm and flexible man who then takes me to a unicorn. We ride them, he has one too, into the sky. Then we become them and I feel the shining point of the horn as a new focal point in my being. I am then back with my parents at the time I was a young boy. I see the gap that exists between me and them. I take my heart and fill this gap with it. That is also how I must fill the gap in my maturation, with my heart. It is good.

CHAPTER 20

THE CARP

On the following day I have another journey. I callout for an animal and a Carp appears. He swims toward me, mouth open. Mouth on my body, then on my penis. I'm embarrassed to tell my human guide this. Carp then tells me to follow him and he swims away. I follow, only then becoming aware that I am in the water.

I'm aware of how slim Carp is, how flexible, how freely and effortlessly he swims. I, on the other hand, feel like I encounter the water broadside (or frontside), not with the skill and smoothness of Carp. I feel like a bulldozer. Carp shows me that there are currents in the water, lines of least resistance. And if one swims along the currents little effort is required.

I then become aware of how I encounter people: I feel obtuse, seemingly doltish or confrontational, abrupt. I meet them head on, or broadside, while Carp seems to dance with people, feeling them fully, easily, warmly.

It suddenly dawns on me that when I meet people I fully expect them to reject me, I anticipate rejection, I am ready for it. I am insensitive to where they are, I don't take the time to become aware of what they are feeling, of what is going on with them. I encounter them with an already formed assessment, coming out of my old injury and panic of the gap. I recognize this also as one aspect of my shyness.

I suddenly remember that I am a Pisces, and that I've always acted as if a part of me is missing. But it is not that something is missing, but that something is present: the callus that I developed to protect me from further injury, the insensitivity to my own needs, is very present in me.

Carp tells me to swim with people.

I feel as if an entire dimension of my life with people awaits me. A way that I must enter into relationships with people. A way that is more like playing. I have been replaying an old injury over and over, I have been creating the callus over and over again in each relationship. Instead I must just begin to swim and play.

The session took about half an hour. One of the simplest, yet most profound, of my experience.

CHAPTER 21

THE ANIMAL OF SOCIAL INJURY

At a training in Germany I am sitting around with the group after supper and we are all chatting. Jokingly I say that whereas some people are mentally retarded, I am socially retarded. I am startled by the fact that no one laughs and so I begin to take my statement seriously. Although I do nothing more about it, it stays very present in my awareness.

About a month later I arrive at Rowe Convention Center where I am scheduled to present a workshop the next day. It is early evening and there will shortly be two hours for meeting casually with the people who will be attending the workshops. I am feeling nervous and so I lie on my bed and ask if there is an animal of social injury that I should meet with.

Immediately a squirrel appears, but he is walking with a crutch and his left rear leg is heavily bandaged. I am aware of how cumbersome it is for him to get around whereas squirrels usually scurry quite rapidly. I ask him what he needs from me and he tells me that

I need to take the bandage off of his leg. I do so. It is an open wound, very raw, there is no skin on most of his leg. He then tells me that I need to touch the wound. I do so, hesitantly and gingerly. As I put my hand on the warm muscle that is exposed and feel both his sensitivity and my own tendency to withdraw from that contact.

As I leave my hand on his wounded leg I have fleeting memories of myself as a child. My father is teaching me how to be social, rigidly instructing me that when I meet someone I am to greet them, shake hands with them, and tell them my name in a formal Spanish way: "Mucho gusto de conocerlo, Estevan Gallegos." Then I am to say nothing more until I am spoken to. As I reflect on this I am aware of my own discomfort and of my father's rigidity, remembering that he only went as far as the third grade in school.

The squirrel then throws away his crutch and begins to scurry around much more easily than before but his left leg is still bent. He is happy that he no longer has to use the crutch and that the heavy bandage is gone, so even though he is not as quick as the other squirrels, he is much more skillful at getting around than he was before. I thank him.

That evening, and throughout the weekend I am deeply struck by how comfortable I feel introducing myself to people at the table and making small talk with them. I am at ease and feel deeply at home with them rather than the awkwardness that I had often felt before.

CHAPTER 22

THE WOMAN IN THE WALKING BED

At a later date when I am again back in Germany, Angela is guiding me through a beautiful relaxation. Suddenly I see a large elephant, waving his trunk in the air and trumpeting loudly, on the edge of a forest. I vaguely see other elephants around him. I approach him and he says, "Finally you've come!" He turns and begins walking through the forest. It soon becomes jungle and as we move through it we come to the ruins of an ancient temple overgrown with weeds and vines. As we move through the ruins we arrive at a stone stairway that leads downward into the deeper structure of this temple. I ask elephant if we should follow it and he says, "Yes, let's see what's down there."

The stairway leads deeper and deeper and I go through a period of confusion, not really knowing where I am nor what is happening. We then arrive at a deeper level and in the distance I see a strange sight: a dark skinned woman is lying on a bed but the bed is walking, each leg of the bed is picking its way very carefully, step by step. As I adjust to this strange sight the bed brings her slowly over to where we are and suddenly a tablecloth is being laid on a small round table and I see that we are being invited for tea. The woman is lying on her peripatetic bed, I have a chair and the elephant also has a chair. Although his chair is the same size as mine it is quite tiny for him and yet he sits on it. I recognize that we are each sitting on something different, The woman is reclining on one elbow on her bed, I am sitting in my chair quite comfortably, and although the elephant's chair is the same size as mine it is very unsuited to him because he is quite large.

The woman turns to me and asks, "What supports you?"

I reply that the chair supports me quite comfortably.

"And what else supports you?", she asks.

As I reflect I recognize that I have many layers of support. Then I suddenly begin to realize that there are ceremonies that support me. The drinking of the tea that we are all engaged in is a ceremony that supports our entering into relationship. I don't know this woman at all and yet this ceremony serves as an entry way into a relationship with her. I then see many, many ceremonies of relationship that are very common, and that we take very much for granted. I also realize that I have never earnestly entered into ceremony, thinking it to be something fake, something false, the putting on of an act but not really the expression of what one felt. But now, seeing it as ceremonies that bring people into relationship with one another it seems quite different, and I realize that I could enter into it fully, almost as a game. I am also aware that we have somehow forgotten that these are ceremonies, and necessary ceremonies, to lighten our interactions and ease the heaviness of one another's company.

The woman then asks me if there are any ceremonies that I do for myself. I search my memory but find none. Then I see a Japanese calligrapher preparing to undertake his calligraphy. He first cleans the room where it will take place, prepares the desk and the brushes, aligns everything quite neatly, and then he ultimately sits down and very deliberately selects a brush.

I then see myself as I choose what I will wear on a particular day. I open a drawer and carefully select which tee shirt I will wear on that day and I realize that these are the rudiments of a ceremony. The woman tells me that having ceremonies for myself will lighten my being, and I realize that it is a way of respecting and honoring one's life.

I feel as if I have been blind about ceremonies, or that there has been a cover over my knowing about them. And I am aware that I never really learned that ceremonies were ceremonies. I felt forced into the few ceremonies that my father taught me and I entered into them with resentment. I also see that if one is to get to know another culture one must really learn all of its ceremonies, for that then gives one a much closer contact with that particular culture.

The elephant is then pouring tea quite elegantly, and I thank him ceremoniously. I then thank the woman for instructing me, and I am playing now, using a British accent.

"Thank you sooo much for instructing me!"

She replies, "Charmed, I'm sure," also playing.

We leave her and return to the stairs, climbing them back up into the ruins of the temple, we go through the jungle and then through the forest, to the place on the edge of the wood where I first met the elephant.

I feel greatly enriched and much, much lighter. The delight of enjoying human relationships awaits me. I thank elephant, ceremoniously.

CHAPTER 23

THE LION FAMILY

At a training in Germany the large group has broken up into smaller groups and I am working in a group of three people. It becomes my turn to journey while one person in the group guides me. The other person is writing whatever I say.

After an enjoyable relaxation I call out for a guide and a Lion immediately jumps out at me. I ask him what he has to tell me and he just licks my face several times. I then ask him what needs to happen and he stands on my supine body and licks my face even more. He then picks me up by the nape of the neck and carries me to his den.

Inside the den are a mother lion and three nursing cubs. I crawl in among the cubs, connect myself to one of her nipples and begin nursing from the mother. The milk is warm and feels beautiful as it enters my body. I am deeply moved. The milk is her love and she is freely pouring her love into us. The Lioness then leans her head around and sniffs me. She begins to lick me. I am completely naked and young. She licks me allover my entire body and there is no part of my body that is ignored or rejected. I feel so totally accepted by her. I feel intimately and fully caressed. I feel deeply, deeply accepted into this family. The lions are just present and completely tangible: the smell, the warmth, the acceptance.

There is no question in the mother's mind. I drink my fill and fall asleep with the other cubs.

The mother then gently disengages from us, goes over to her mate and he licks her face. She then leaves the den. The male lion positions himself at the entry way. He lies there completely relaxed but totally alert. His presence is awesomely reassuring. It is obvious that his entire power is available for the protection of the cubs, me included.

The mother goes into the jungle, sleek, alert, graceful. Her eye is keen but it is really smell that tells her what is in the forest. She experiences its entire extent by smell. Through smell the forest is transparent to her, whereas by sight she can only see until something blocks her view.

Mother lion trots briskly until she is some distance from the den. I can feel the male lion's complete trust in her, and her complete trust in him. She becomes suddenly still, alert. Her ears twitch. She gently sniffs the air. She then begins to move stealthily, creeping, her body close to the earth. She smells the warmth of a nearby rabbit. Lightening fast she springs, grasps the rabbit in her mouth and breaks its neck. She then relaxes, taking her time to consume the rabbit, its fur, blood, bones, muscles, guts. The rabbit is delicious, tasty, warming, nurturing. She feels it warmly in her belly. She licks her lips and slowly makes her way back to her den, although she is still very alert.

She enters the den and the male lion smells her and licks her head and neck as she enters. He can smell the rabbit she has eaten. She licks each cub and me as well, and then lies among us once again, making her nipples available to us.

I feel a deep, deep sense of family; of safety; of the presence of the parents: strong, full, healthy. The cubs are completely strong, with no fear whatsoever. They feel totally safe. I realize this is the first completely healthy family I have ever experienced. I know now, for the first time in my life, what it is like to live in a healthy family. It is so natural, so completely simple.

The male lion then picks me up once again by the scruff of the neck, carries me out of the den and into the forest where he leaves me. I lie on the forest floor, on the earth, feeling a deep appreciation the healthy family that I have just visited. I realize how injured my own parents were. I see my mother as severely injured, perhaps 50% present. The rest of her is an injured child. My father is perhaps 30% present. The rest of him is an injured child. I see there was possibility of us having a healthy family, were very injured when young. To have a family they would have had to have healed. I realize that there is probably no human child growing up in a totally healthy family.

As I lie on the earth I suddenly realize that the earth is my healthy mother and that the surrounding jungle is my healthy father. My mother nurses me and my father stands sentinel. They accept me fully. They tell me they will be there forever, my mother nursing and nurturing me and my father standing vigilant. I feel finally healthy.

CHAPTER 24

THE HEALING PLACE

MYTHOLOGY

The term "mythology" has come to have several meanings. On the one had it has come to mean something that is untrue, false, confabulated. On the other hand we know mythology to be a collection of literary stories that we attribute to ancient cultures and presume that these were their beliefs. But ever since Joseph Campbell was hosted by Bill Moyers on Public television the interest in mythology has taken on a new resurgence. Joseph Campbell spent his life in the comparative study of myths from different times and cultures.

He came to three conclusion about myths:

- That they were a way of teaching the mind how to become realigned with the body when the mind had gone off on its own tangents.
- That myths were maps to help people as they grew through the different stages of their lives.
- That myths were reflections of the ways cultures related to having been hunters or growers.

Carl Jung had pursued the study of the similarities between the themes of ancient myths and the spontaneous arisings from the depths of the mind in dreams, in artistic creations, and in the fantasies of mental patients.

We study the myths of various cultures as if they emanate somehow to form the common heritage of that culture but we do not ask the vital questions: Where do myths arise from? How do they begin? And why?

My own work with people helping them develop a relationship with the deepest aspects of their own imagery process has taught me it is not enough to just study mythology. What we have taken to be mythology is but an archeology of the deep experiences of human beings who lived long ago. It is not enough to just do a comparative study, to intellectually look at mythology. We are just dusting off dead bones. True mythology must be a personal experience, an experience with such depth that it shakes us to the core. Its intention is to change us, to grow us, to help us become someone that we are not yet.

It is true that when we truly experience our own mythology we encounter themes and dimensions that others have encountered before, and it is an entertaining exercise to compare these events across persons, but that is not the purpose of mythology. It was not intended to be a scholastic exercise.

In Alchemical writings we encounter many different themes, some of which we could even call universal. But that is only to say that most people have two legs. I do not sit around all day intellectualizing about the fact that my two legs are very similar to those of other people. I need to walk, run, dance, crawl, hop, jump, skip, limp, straddle, kick, and much more in order for my legs to be of and for me to be in a living relationship with them.

The same is true for mythology. It does not come play through my intellectual study of The theme of the alchemical marriage, or the hieros gamos, is abundantly present in alchemical writings and in the writings of Carl Jung. But however much I read about them it does not affect my inner state. Additionally I cannot dictate the time for the marriage to occur. All I can do is to continue my growing and my own healing, and to welcome the event when it does occur.

THE PATH JOURNEY

I am visiting my friend Christian in Switzerland following a training. I am aware of an intense energy within me and I ask if he will guide me on a journey. Lying on the couch I close my eyes and call out within myself for a guide. I am quite astonished that no guide appears, but there is a path before me. As I set myself upon the path Christian suggests that I ask the path if it is my guide.

It answers immediately, saying, "I have always been your guide! Follow me!"

The path is a dirt path, the setting is quite lovely, in the country. I walk along the path, enjoying the summer day and then I find myself suddenly in a little bakery in Switzerland. I recognize the shop and try to remember when I was here before: it was after I had guided Christian on a journey up on Rigi Mountain. Upon our return to Lucerne we had stopped at this bakery. I recognize the deep feeling of friendship that I feel toward my friend, Christian.

Then I am walking along the path again. I have a sense that there are important places along this path rather than it going toward a specific goal. I think how warm and supportive Christian is. It is the kind of friendship I would have liked to have had with my father. I then see other past friendships I have had and the warmth and beauty of each, and I realize that my path has always been warm and friendly.

I realize that I have always viewed my life as having been cold and lonely and rejecting, but now I am seeing that I have always had friends, loving friends, and I wonder why I had been looking at my life in such austere terms. I then begin wondering if it involved my rejecting others, rather than my being rejected, my rejecting others but blaming them for the rejection.

I then see how I rejected my father, after he whipped me. I see also the time that I rejected my mother, coldly, unforgivingly. It had come after she had engaged me in a discussion when I was a child. She was asking me things about my father, and after much coaxing I told her that I was very afraid of him and I asked her not to tell him that. She agreed not to tell him. However, that night, when they were both in bed, I overheard her asking him to be more gentle with me, telling him that I was afraid of him. I was stunned. She had deliberately done what I had asked her not to. The next morning, and perhaps from then on, I was bitterly cold toward her.

Am I so filled with rejection?

The path replies: "No, you are just very good at it. Yes, you have been rejected and you have participated in rejection."

I see how unyielding I have been in my rejecting, how utterly determined I have been in it. I recognize what an utterly determined child I was! I remember a snowball fight in the fourth or fifth grade, when two groups of boys were throwing snowballs at each other, and how gradually, one by one, boys left the side I was on and went over to the other side, until I was the only one left on my side and I started throwing mud-balls. I was determined that I would never switch sides, never! I was totally determined, entrenched in my determination. I can see that I also took that stance with my father: I became totally rejecting of him. That has been a major polarity in my life: totally giving love or totally rejecting.

The path tells me that I have always seen how the world loved or rejected me, but now it is time to see how I did that too: how my loving or rejecting was active in my being loved or rejected. The path tells me that I entered into it with such an intensity that I have been totally unaware of the power of my rejecting nature or the power of my capacity to love. And that my unwillingness to approach someone for fear of being rejected was itself a form of rejection of them, an anticipatory rejection.

I then begin seeing the little kid that I was, so intense in his love and in his rejection, so determined. He is an angry little kid, so angry. He's saying: "I'll kill the whole world!" He doesn't want to feel the hurt that is there.

I approach him slowly, carefully. He says to me: "I'll kill you! I'll kill you!"

I reach him and put my arms around him. His whole back is bruised and bloody. He needs someone to take care of him. He is so unwilling to trust me to do that. He is deeply into his anger. His back is just a mess. He doesn't want to focus his awareness there because it hurts too much. He is just fighting for his life, saying: "I don't care if I die, I'll kill him first!"

I just hold him, saying to him over and over, "You have been so hurt, you have been so hurt." He begins to focus his awareness on the hurt instead of just on the anger. I then begin to see situations where my father tried to help heal the old wounds: by taking me hunting, by restoring cars and giving them to me, by trying to say nice things to me, but the hurt was always there. I never even took into consideration how he tried to heal things, the original hurt was so deep!

The boy is sobbing now, saying: "I hurt! I hurt!"

I suddenly realize how small this kid is, how tiny he is! He's just a tiny little kid, only four years old!

I ask him: "What do you need from me?"

He says: "I want you to love me again!"

The word "again" startles me. I suddenly realize that I have rejected him all my life because he has been so angry! I hadn't even realized I had been rejecting him!

He says: "Will you love me when I'm angry?" I suddenly understand that my rejection of him in his anger was a large part of my withdrawing when I got angry at someone! I tell him that I will love him even when he's angry.

He says: "My anger is true! My anger is righteous!"

He had been hurt so deeply that any hint of more hurt would bring up that anger. He speaks like a little knight. I suddenly feel things moving, shifting, changing. The whole landscape is changing.

I see him going up to his sister after both he and she have been whipped, feeling warm and loving toward her, with a sense of common destiny, but she is very angry at him and lashes out at him: "If you hadn't run out in front of that car I wouldn't have gotten whipped!" He feels as if he had lost his last and only friend!

He and I are sitting there watching the scene. I tell him: "I will be your friend!"

I see his sister getting up off the bench where she has been lying on her stomach and she is happy again. Mother and father are there too. It is as if they had all been in a play: "Oh, wasn't that intense!" As if they had all been playing roles. The boy is leery but then he melts and they all talk as a cast of a play would talk after their grand performance. Father says: "I didn't know I could hit that hard." The boy says to the sister: "You got angry at me." The sister says: "Let's do it again." The boy says: "No, let's not." They all got caught up in their roles really seriously. I see myself moving toward them and then I suddenly find myself walking along the path again.

I have changed somehow but I don't know how. The path says: "Yes, our experiences change us!" I'm aware now that I had never gone through that experience completely. I don't know how I'm different but I am.

The path says: "You'll discover it as you go along." I continue along the path now, jauntily, whistling. I walk for a while and then I notice that there are some cultivated fields on both sides of the path. There is a small cozy-looking village ahead. The people in the fields are ending their work for the day and are beginning to move toward the village. They are warm and content, very friendly. Their activity is all related to the earth and toward doing those things that directly provide their own nurturing. They have a direct relationship to the source of their nurturing.

There is a warmth in them as there is in the earth. As we get closer to the village more and more of them join in and I am accepted fully by them. I ask them where they are going. They tell me there is a wedding going on in the village.

I remember an occasion when I was first in Germany in my twenties. A group of people in a bar invited me to join them. I was completely suspicious, thinking they were going to take advantage of me, or that they wanted something from me. I could not just experience their friendship.

We all arrive in the village square. It is an ancient village with half-timbered houses. I ask the man standing next to me:

"Who's getting married?"

He replies: "Why, you are!"

I then ask: "Who am I marrying?"

He says, "Why, you're marrying yourself!"

I feel the sense of some strange taboo.

I see the bride and groom She is beautiful, dark skinned, wearing a white wedding gown, smaller than the groom. He is much younger than I, formally dressed in a tuxedo, with a much lighter complexion than she. He has dark hair.

A portly gentleman in a top hat emerges. He is possibly the mayor. He announces that it is time for the wedding. Everyone cheers.

I feel that the woman carries much of the little boy in her, perhaps the anger and that tremendous tenacity. The groom seems rather bland.

I am watching them as a member of the crowd, but I am also the bride and also the groom. The path has now become the town square. I suddenly realize that all the women I have fallen in love with carried something of that angry little boy in them. I have been trying to have a relationship with that little boy through these women, trying to form that marriage in my everyday life, when I needed to form it in myself!

The mayor in the top hat then says: "Do you, Stephen Gallegos, take this bride, Stephen Gallegos, to be your lawfully wedded wife?"

The groom answers, "Yes, I do."

"Do you, Stephen Gallegos, take this groom, Stephen Gallegos, to be your lawfully wedded husband?"

The bride answers, "Yes, I do."

I can feel the little kid deep down inside her belly. He says: "It's about time!"

So they/we embrace and kiss. She is who I have been searching for all my life in other women! There is also something deeply mysterious about her!I wonder to myself, "How will we get along?"

She replies: "Just great!"

The entire town celebrates! It is a good little town. I feel for the first time part of a community. I am aware that I could never really belong to a community until there was this kind of communion in myself! I feel something coming together very deep inside my chest.

There is a troupe in the village putting on a play using the back of a wagon as a stage. It is a play about a little kid who is always full of spunk, who is always into everything, always in trouble— father, mother, and sister are there—the kid loves it. They all take a bow. The town loves it. It feels like a play that has all been going on in me. I have been assuming it was real.

The bride and groom are sitting together and are joined in some way, at the shoulder.

The whole community then accompanies them to their new home. I am part of this company. It is a very nice house at the edge of town on a little hill. All the lights in it are burning brightly. It is not a single style of architecture but seems to contain all styles within itself. The path says: "Go in and look at your new home!" I go through the door. I'm not sure who I am. I'm all four of these people, the bride, the groom, the little boy, and myself that is in the audience.

Inside the house is brightly lit and it is strange. There are two distinct natures to the house simultaneously: it is on the one hand a single open room with nothing in it, no furniture, nothing. But it is completely illuminated, very bright, a large, large chamber. On the other hand, wherever I turn there is a special room: a cozy little room for reading, with a comfortable chair, a nice lamp and table, good books.

A special room for meeting people. A larger room for social gatherings. A lovely kitchen. A large area for crafts. Guest rooms. They all appear and then disappear as I go by.

The bedroom is on the upper floor. It is the only room on that upper floor. We go up the stairs leading to it. It is surrounded by windows overlooking the village and the countryside. The bride and groom enter it. We/I enter it and go stand at the window.

The entire community is down below clapping. I am then a member of the audience down below looking up at the window. The bride and groom are waving, then they close the curtains. The crowd, me among them, cheers and goes back to the village square to continue their celebration. We all sit at little tables in the square and drink.

The square is paved with cobblestones, the houses around are distinct and unique. I see that there are four or five streets leading into the square, entering through archways or between houses. I ask the path where these streets lead to. The path answers: "All these streets have led you here!" I ask the path: "What now?" "Celebrate! Celebrate!"

There are tables surrounding the square with people sitting at them; people are eating and dancing. I ask the square what it needs from me. It replies: "Keep me well polished, and be aware that I will always guide you."

I realize that I need to have an ongoing relationship with it, a relationship of respect, of reverence. We look up at the house on the hill. The light goes off in the bedroom. All the people cheer and go back to celebrating.

Slowly, gradually, I return.

THIS is mythology. My mythology. It speaks to me personally. I feel it deeply. It comes to me at the appropriate time, as both a passageway and a way marker. Now I know where I am in myself, now I know better who it is that I am. No amount of intellectual reading about alchemy could have taken me to the place that this journey has brought me to. There is no way that I could have created this experience intellectually. This dimension where the imagery occurs spontaneously and invites my interaction is truly the healing place. And it is a place that exists within each human being.

In truth we have been so preoccupied with the outer aspects of mythology that we have failed to realize that it is the inner, the subjective, dimension of mythology that is the potent healing place in each individual. The journey, once told, is what we take mythology to be. But the myth came forth spontaneously in a human being before it ever became a story told. And it came forth for the purposes of healing and growing that individual; it was a specific, unique, personal experience.

We live in an age where the unique subjectivity of each individual has been so eroded that we have even recently gone through a period of time when we were convinced that it didn't exist, or even if it did, it didn't matter because there was no way to objectively validate it and subject it to scientific verification.

What hubris! The existence of mythology has always pointed to the fact of the existence of the healing place, and to the essential nature of the unique individual subjective experience as the most vital dimension possible.

Each one of us must go deeply into our own mythology. It awaits us. It is the only path that fully heals and grows us!

THE HEALING OF MY WOUNDEDNESS

I was conducting a training in the Personal Totem Pole Process in Ireland. The group was halfway through its second year of meeting for two separate weeks each year. The group, interestingly, consisted of thirteen women and I was the only man, and they were doing beautiful work. At one of the afternoon discussion sessions one of the participants was commenting on a childhood injury and I remarked offhandedly that the injury was not so severe. She became incensed at me for making such a casual remark about something that was so deep and personal to her, and I could well understand her position, but nonetheless, the thought still came to me that much worse things had happened to many other people. I was curious about my lightness of attitude especially in the face of her seriousness. At this point one of the other participants suggested that perhaps I needed to journey to meet with my original wounded-ness. I agreed.

I asked one of the powerful women if she would guide me, and asked another who happened to be a midwife if she would scribe my session. The others then broke up into groups of three or four to do their own journeying. The following journey occurred:

Once I have been taken through the relaxation, my guide invites me to call out and ask if an animal of my wounded-ness could come be with me. I do so and immediately a voice within me says that it is the animal of my healed-ness that I should meet. A large bear, looking like a very large beige teddy bear, appears.

I ask the bear what needs to happen here and he reaches out his arms as if to hold me. I find myself immediately an infant in my mother's lap. She is sitting in a rocking chair in the living room of the adobe house where I was born. It is late evening and there is a fire burning in the stove. I remember this stove from my childhood; it had sheets of mica in the openings of the front grate. I was always fascinated by the translucence of the mica and by its organic quality. It was not like the glass in windows nor was it like anything else that I knew. This stove was the only place where I had ever seen it.

My guide invites me to greet the mica and so I say hello to it and I ask it what needs to happen. The mica answers: you need to see through me and then you'll know.

I am sitting on the floor in front of the stove. There is a warmth from my mother who is in the rocking chair next to me. The mica flickers with the glow of the fire on the other side and I stare intently at it. I begin to see images in it and am reminded of my childhood. As a child wherever I looked I would see images. At night when I looked at the wall next to my bed I would see all kinds of faces in that wall.

I say to the mica "There are images in you." The mica answers "Good, you are beginning." I say to the mica "I presume I carry those images within me and project them onto you." The mica replies "What else do you see?" I reply "I see the fire that is on the other side of you." The mica answers "Good. What else do you see?"

I become aware that I am an obstacle in front of the stove and that I need to see through myself as well. I then experience myself as an awareness behind my head. My head feels thick and obtuse. I see the back of my head and the hair and the skin. I see inside my head: the blood vessels and brain. I am aware thatI am seeing things I have only learned about since I know I have never seen the inside of my head. I realize that I am being asked to look through what I have learned. I suddenly become aware of a feeling running through my ears and jaw; it is a feeling of anger or ferociousness.

As I focus on the feeling I feel the snarling snout of a dog or wolf—the sharp teeth and curling lip. I experience this as my own, protruding in front of my face. A shudder suddenly runs through me as I realize that this was an entire dimension of my childhood that had been forbidden! I was not allowed to experience these aspects of myself. Whenever these aspects appeared in me I was severely judged and reprimanded by my parents. I realize that these were aspects my parents did not allow themselves either.

Dog, who has now appeared, shows me that these feelings arose mostly when I was with other children: challenging them, holding and honoring my own space, feeling proud and experiencing my power. My parents counseled me to be weak, to give in to the other child, to give up whatever the other child wanted. I felt my parents were always shutting me up, closing me down, disallowing those dimensions of myself that would naturally set boundaries, and whenever I was with my parents I would feel an opposition to what was natural in my being.

I then see the dog interacting with other dogs. First they bark at each other, then they slowly approach one another and sniff, ultimately they play. I realize that my parents disallowed those initial aspects of the encounter; they expected immediate play without permitting the challenges and exploration that were natural antecedents to the play. When I did play with other children I felt disempowered because of the lack of the initial challenge. Dog shows me that when I was with new kids I'd feel the presence of my parents in my jaw, like an ache, and the thought would come that I was supposed to be a good little boy. Even when my parents were not present I would feel them there, observing, judging, criticizing. I feel an earache and a hatred of my parents, an injury that was always present when I was with other people. I felt that injury when I would play sports or do anything else that involved other people, and I recognize that it is a basic component of my shyness, of my holding back.

Dog has now become a wolf. He is running along in the wilderness, hearing, smelling, seeing. He is completely at home in that wilderness. I see the scene from above. The house in which I was born and grew up, that small adobe house that my father had built, surrounded by fields and trees and a large irrigation ditch running some distance behind it. Wolf runs free in the wilderness that surrounds my childhood home.

I also see how tight my house was as a child. How closed and confining it was. To wolf it would have been a prison. Wolf is trotting along, secure and free, and I see that his wilderness should have been my home as well. I recognize that all that I was taught to fear is really the home of the natural wolf, and the house that I was taught was safe was in fact a prison and the most dangerous place in my life as a child.

I recall scenes of going off with my good friend, Orlando Valenzuela, into the surrounding hills on horseback, exploring what was then still very much wilderness. I see how much my friend gave me of his world, and how little I brought to him but friendship.

Wolf has changed now into a coyote: wily, secretive, hidden. I ask coyote what I need to know from him and he immediately takes me to his den, his burrow. Inside are his mate and her two cubs. Coyote invites me to enter and I crawl into the den. I smell the strong smell of coyote which fills the den and then I abruptly realize that there are many smells inside the den: the smell of the cubs, the smell of coyote's mate, the smell of the cubs nursing, the smell of urine, the smell of the damp earth, the smell of roots that protrude through the ceiling. I am aware of how infinitely accepting the coyotes are and that they don't consider me an intruder. Then I become aware of my own smell in that den. Both of the adults sniff me: my feet, my crotch, my face and ears. I ask the male coyote if I can become him in order to experience myself as he does. He agrees and I merge into him as he sniffs my body. I realize that to him I am a landscape of smells. He knows me through and through with his olfactory way of seeing. There is no place on my body that he avoids, no place is taboo, no place not to be seen or smelled.

I become aware of how we humans hide our smells, with deodorants and perfumes, how we disguise our naturalness. We hide our ability to smell by smoking or burning incense, we hide our ability to know. I see how rich coyote's world is, how accessible, and how available he is to that world.

I tell coyote I will come out of him now and he then invites me to merge into his mate so that I can experience their world through her. I merge into her and am immediately aware of her belly. As she nurses her cubs I become aware that she experiences each cub as part of herself, and she pours her own being into them, freely, in the form of her milk. She sniffs them and licks them all over, cleaning them with her tongue. No part of them disgusts her. She feels a beautiful warmth toward them both.

I am suddenly aware of myself as an infant. I am lying on top of the basinette. My mother is washing me, changing me, powdering me. I feel her full lovingness. I feel how for her I was an extension of her body. I experience the continuity between us. She was my warmth, she filled me inside as I did her, she kept me safe, soft. There was no concern with survival, I was just a being experiencing that caring.

She took care of all my needs, of making sure that I was safe and warm and fed. My existence was just one of being, of being fed, of being held, of being changed. She was devoted and loving, anticipating my needs. I experience the pride and happiness that she felt toward me. There was no need for me to be any different than I was. I felt deeply, deeply held.

Suddenly I find myself shrieking with pain! My entire infant body is convulsing in shock. I am in a doctor's office being circumcised without an anesthetic and the pain is unbearable. My entire body tries to contract away from the pain. It feels like I am being killed! Where is that mother of whom I am apart? Why is she not here protecting me? How could she allow this to happen? There is a sense of total disbelief that this could come about! Every cell in my body is convulsing in shock and pain! I FEEL MYSELF DEEPLY NEEDING TO BE COMFORTED and at the same time very wary, my life is being threatened, seriously, totally, and she is not there to protect me. It feels like I am being cut away from her.

I see the two coyote parents watching this scene from above. They are frantic, running back and forth, trying to get to that injured child but unable to, needing to protect it, not comprehending at all how his mother could let this happen.

I see my mother sitting in the waiting room next to where the circumcision is being performed, full of doubt but rationalizing that the earlier this was done the better, that it would involve less pain, that it was medically justified. Not realizing that to the child this is an incomprehensible event that came way too early in his life if it needed to come at all.

I then see that there is a residue of that event in me involving mistrust, suspicion, wariness. It never healed. A division between me and other people, and the way my parents would not let me mark my territory fed into that old injury. I see myself growing up in an insulated way around people. I was okay with animals and plants but I was insulated to people.

There was always that questioning as well as a heightened sensitivity to injury and a not trusting. I see that at school I became deadened to the fact that the insulation was there. I see the two coyotes watching the little baby. He still hurts, his whole body hurts, every cell is in a state of alarm.

Then a deep resentment towards the mother develops for allowing that to happen. There is a confusion in him. He needs her so badly exactly because of that wounding. That is a place that has persisted in my life: both resenting her and needing her. And it is an event that has been present in my three marriages and all my relationships with women: resentment and need.

I see the coyotes heading back toward their burrow now, they nod and return, and say that there will now be another guide for me. I see the house where I was born, way out in the country, and the wariness of being hurt again, and being taught that the wilderness was the dangerous place. My fear and injury was projected out into the wilderness, the wilderness was the dangerous place. That fear and injury got shoved out into the wilderness, yet I know now that the wilderness was the safe place and that people hurt me for their own reasons. So there is an underlying distrust of people who profess to know what is good for me, justifying their actions, and it delayed my journey of finding the animals, of coming back to a knowing I could trust.

I then see myself at the time when I was being weaned, both needing and resenting. I yearn so for the breast! What can I do to bring back the nurturing I need? We are on a long car journey to Albuquerque. I am cross and hungry so my mother nurses me one more time just to quiet me. I am unbelieving. What had I done that brought the nursing back? I need to know! I frantically need to know!

I see that my mother felt guilty for the early circumcision and tried to make up for it in my early life by being overly attentive.

Then I see myself at a time when she was pregnant with my little sister, Rosalie. The scene is again the living room in the house where I was born. My mother is sitting in the rocking chair in front of the stove. My father is also in the room, reading. I want to sit in my mother's lap. She asks my father if he can't do something with me, implying that perhaps he could hold me in his lap. My father says to me gruffly: you're a big boy now, you don't need to sit in a lap anymore! I feel further rejection and resentment, and a deep need to be held. I see that there was a deep confusion in me around needing. I resented myself for being so needy. I should be grown up already and not needing. I feel that I was yanked out of growing as a process; growing was already supposed to have happened, I was somehow already supposed to be grown. I see in my life how I have come to honor the process of growing and how my major function in the world has become to help people become aware of their own growing and of their need for that growth.

I had not been aware that I had come to resent the neediness in myself. Within myself I apologize to my neediness for having resented it so. My neediness replies that it was just a way of growing. I had come to view it like an enemy. I see that my present celibacy is part of that confusion: neediness as being frozen around that early injury. Neediness has to do with relationship and needs to be respected; it is a gift. The injury of the early circumcision has injured my relationships with people, the franticness felt like a matter of life or death.

Now I see Connie. I fell deeply in love with her when I was eighteen years old. She recently died of cancer. I had visited her six weeks before she died. I was always aware of how deeply I loved her. She was my holy grail. It was a love that was beyond neediness. She says to me: "Just love!" and as she says this I see that my love for her never got confused with neediness, with my franticness.

That confusion in which I lived so much of my life involved so many different things: the need for trust and a mistrust of trusting those you love most, intense pain and the most serious threat to my physical existence I have ever experienced, a fear of needing and of honoring my needs as valid, a deep rage around people doing things "for your own good" but without my consent! My entire life has been a quest to sort out the dimensions that came into being with that original injury. I see that love was totally present initially in my life, and that I was originally deeply at home in the world. The circumcision was so injurious, a jarring that intruded into the holiness of being. My whole being surrounded that injury like an abscess it wanted to understand and resolve to a place of healing.

I see the giant teddy bear and he transforms into my original heart bear. Inside of him is another teddy bear, a teddy bear I had as a child. I see coyote safe and protected with his family. I see my mother in the hospital before she died. She says to me: "All one can do is trust." She is deeply pleased at how this injury has healed. I realize she felt my injury as much as I did, and I realize that this is what a mother does. I see my father. He says: "I didn't know how to help you be a man." He felt confused by my confusion, my resentment, my franticness. He felt it in himself and he also didn't know how to make demands.

Neediness says: "Let me see clearly in yourself and in other people, you don't have to satisfy the need but you do need to know it is there."

I realize that when I have been around people who were needy I felt my resentment. Resentment and neediness have been bound together in my life but now they can once again be separate. Neediness was part of my power. It wanted to save me during the circumcision and it then remained present in a frozen way. It tells me that it needs to melt. I can feel it in my left hand, melting and draining into my heart.

I ask love if there is anything that needs to happen and it says: "Just stay present." I feel a light coming into my heart and head and into the snarling dog who needed his boundaries, a knowing that needs to be honored. I feel the light in my hands and down through the rest of my body. It feels so simple. I feel how the light was nurtured by my friend Orlando, and I also feel how my second wife tried to kill it. A voice says: "Remember your trust!"

I suddenly realize that this circumcision that took place when I was less than a week old set the path of my life: It was the injury whose healing I sought! It was the injury that severely disturbed my relationships with people. It was the injury that brought me to distrust outer solutions and carried me until I met the inner animals, the place of resolution that comes from within, personally, individually, uniquely. My mother had been treating me like a statistic and my need was to return to the uniqueness of my being human! Seeing all of this I thank the circumcision for setting my life's path, even though thanking it feels like a strange thing to do. Through it the power and the love guided me. I also thank my mother and my father.

I return from the journey feeling thankful for my life's path and for the healing that has just happened.

Suddenly my whole life makes sense.

During the night following the session just described I have difficulty sleeping. I experience a hard place in my head and jaw and focus my attention there. I suddenly have the realization that my father was not circumcised. Circumcision was not a part of his culture. The circumcision was obviously only my mother's idea!!! And I remember a time, I must have been five or six years old, when she was speaking of circumcision and I asked her if I had been circumcised. I shuddered when she replied, "Yes, you were circumcised, but it was done at an early age when babies don't feel anything." I then understood where the casualness of my remark to the woman in my training had come from!

My own circumcision was a barbaric act performed in the name of rationality and science, although there is no reason and no science that can justify injuring a child who is only a few days old.

When my daughter was born one of the nurses wanted to take some blood from her by piercing her heel. The nurse said: "They don't feel anything at this age!" Our educational system instills such stupidity, but only after the nurse's own awareness has been stunted, probably beginning with a similar injury perpetrated upon her at an early age.

Among the Maasai people in Africa circumcision is used as a passageway, but this is very different from inflicting it upon an infant. The rite is performed on all boys between twelve and fourteen in a social ceremony following a lengthy preparation. The boys are aware it is going to take place and it is viewed as a sacred ceremony through which the boy will enter manhood. The boy himself must sharpen the knives that will be used, and he must select his most trusted male friend to hold him during the ceremony. He is to show bravery and not to wince or cry out. If he does it is considered shameful for his entire family. So the boy must develop the ability to embrace the experience, the pain, the fear, the terror, he must embrace this all within his awareness and it is through the embracing of this experience that his energy is shunted to a new level, that of being a man and no longer a boy. The boundaries of the experience that he can encompass with his awareness are thus greatly stretched and broadened. It is a serious and valuable passageway for him, and one in which his own preparation is vital and essential.

In our culture we have used circumcision not as a passageway from boyhood to manhood, but as the first injury which then keeps the boy a boy, untrusting of the other members of his culture.

Several weeks after my healing experience I was driving with my daughter in the countryside around Santa Fe. There was a blazing red sunset and as we drove through the beautiful land I felt a deep love for my daughter, but I also felt a deep sadness at the same time. As I focused on the feelings I recognized the sadness as the remaining feeling from my early injury, and I saw that I had carried that sadness with me throughout my life, and that I had always tried to wring an understanding from the immediate situation as to what the sadness was about. Then I understood: it was an original sadness that I had never understood, the sadness of having been cut away from my mother so early, and a sadness that I could now lay to rest. I need carry it with me no longer.

Since this final laying to rest I have felt very different. Something that was always present in my life is now no longer there. I feel a deep contentment and a pervasive presence and I see how everything in the world makes sense if we are only willing to let it grow us fully.

CHAPTER 26

JOURNEY TO THE CENTER OF THE UNIVERSE

I call out for a guide and a lanky powerful leopard comes. I ask what needs to happen and Leopard picks me up by the nape of the neck and carries me up a stone mountain. We sit at the pinnacle and survey the surrounding landscape. For as far as we can see there are vast valleys, rich and blossoming, verdant mountains, a slight mist. It is awesome, magnificent, beautiful. I ask if there is something I should know about it. Leopard says to me: this all belongs to you! I look around and have difficulty thinking of it as belonging to me. My mind is flipping around in what ownership is and I tell Leopard that I have difficulty acknowledging it as belonging to me.

Upon hearing these words Leopard immediately takes me by the nape of the neck again, leaps into a treetop and down onto the earth. We travel to a nearby river which I think of as small but as we near it I see that it is a raging river, churning, extremely powerful. I ask Leopard what its source is and he tells me that I don't need to know that. I ask what needs to happen and Leopard says we need to swim. It looks way too powerful to me for us to swim in it but we both dive in. I am amazed to find that under the churning white surface it is peaceful and clear, It is also luminous.

We can swim underneath and there is no need to surface in order to breathe. I ask what we're to do there and Leopard answers: swim.

I realize this is like my life. When something seems too powerful for me to deal with I need to go deeper, and beneath it will be clear and illuminated.

We then come to a large basin. Leopard and I are tiny compared to the size of the basin, and not only does the water continue along the river bed, but here it also goes downward, and we begin to follow it downward. We are swimming deep, deep into the earth. I have never gone so deep before. Leopard says: come, come! We continue to swim deeper and deeper until suddenly we are out in the Universe. I think to myself: I know this place! It feels safe and familiar.

And I think: perhaps on my journey home the plane will fall into the ocean and I will emerge in the Universe. There is nothing to fear. Leopard says: come, come! We eventually come to what feels like the center of the Universe. It is dense and white and luminous. Leopard takes me through the boundary and deeper into it still. It is so large that Leopard and I are like specks of dust in it.

Suddenly a large voice says: What do you want here?

Leopard says: I bring my friend who has recently gotten married! The voice then says to me: what do you want. I say I have come to grow. The voice says: when you have done growing the only thing to do is to be. It then asks me if I am ready to die. I say that I am, and truthfully feel completely prepared to die, and truly don't know if I will die this very moment. It is remarkably peaceful.

I then find myself back on the mat and filled with the white light from the center of the Universe. As I lie there I become aware that the white light itself knows what to do and things are very simple. There is nothing that I need to know. My arms move very, very slowly and I sit up and lie back down, all very, very slowly. There is absolutely no effort. The white light seemed not only to be present but also felt like it extended back in time to the beginnings of the Universe.

I then see myself as a young man (when I still had hair) stumbling around blindly, wandering, not knowing where he was going. But I also saw that he was searching and that his search was bringing him little by little toward me. And I just lie there and wait (although it felt like I was standing) and very, very gradually he comes closer and closer until suddenly he is engulfed in the white light that fills me.

I feel that Leopard is separate from me but somehow also a part of me. I ask Leopard what needs to happen now and as I ask that, I realize I know what needs to happen. I open my eyes very slowly and return.

CHAPTER 27

ONLY PASSAGEWAYS

My wife, Mary (Diggin), is guiding me. I see below me, underwater, a sea monster or a giant catfish. I ask it what needs to happen and it tells me to jump in. I ask if it means into the water and it replies "Of course!!!" I am slightly annoyed by the demand implied in its answer, but I allow myself to descend into the water.

We both float slowly downward, it is facing me, and I look like I am the size of a worm. As we descend I go through numerous memories of my childhood.

It is evening. My father has fixed supper for me and my young sister, Rosalie. My mother has driven to Albuquerque where she is attending evening classes at the university. Juliet has gone with her. I do something that upsets my father and he whips me. I start to cry. My father, after whipping me, tells me that if I don't stop crying he will whip me again. Since the crying is just flowing out of me I don't know how to stop crying, but through intense effort I force myself into silence.

I feel now that something became frozen in my jaw and neck at that time. I see places of frozenness and resistance in me, and around me. I see that my father commanded attention through my fear of him, and that whenever he was around I was focussed not on my experience but on those things that might possibly bring his wrath down upon me. I see just how much of my life has been built upon avoidance.

The catfish and I descend further and further into the water. The giant catfish invites me to look below. I see a bottom layer that is black and I presume it is death. As we descend into the black layer it feels spongy and we continue on through it.

I have the sudden revelation that no destination is final, that all targets are themselves only passageways and that there is nothing fixed in this world, or in the universe. I begin to see that my very body is only a passageway, and with this I begin to relax, there is nothing to fear. I see that we make things static through avoiding them, that we freeze things through naming and describing them, that I fix myself into an identity for the sake of others, and this keeps me from living in my own depths.

It feels as if my entire body is melting, as if the world around me is melting, I see how I have lived in terms of fixed goals and static things, and how all is really only passageways. I see how I am a passageway for others, and also how some people have tried to fix me into something static rather than focusing on their own passageway.

I arise from the journey feeling very different, as if somehow I have been living in a false world, but a world of my own making. I feel how I have frozen the fluidity of the passageway world, and also how I have frozen myself into a fixed being, rather than allowing the fluidity of the passageway that I myself am.

CHAPTER 28

THE LITTLE BLACK BOY

Sometime later, I began having glimpses of a little boy, the black little boy, who at one time swore that he would kill his parents, swore that he would kill the world. I was surprised to see him so hidden away, so tucked away, hiding, not wanting to be seen, feeling guilty at his own existence. And I knew that not only had he hidden himself away, but that I also had hidden him, that I felt guilty about his existence, and wanted unknowingly to hide him in the deepest corner possible. And I also saw how he was the polarity of who I had become. In his wanting to kill the world, I had gone out to heal the world. In his wanting to kill his parents, I had gone out into the world to heal parents and to help them understand and love their children, to help them treat their children with respect. I recognized the polarity that I had become in order to balance and compensate for his existence. And I see how the confusion that I had always felt was a confusion about our existence within the same being, and our trying to split that being apart.

And so I turned to this little black boy and welcomed him, greeted him, and took him in my arms. For a long, long time we just held each other, I giving him the love that he so desperately wanted and needed, and he bringing me the power and the balance that I have so desperately sought all my life, and the ultimate understanding.

I realized that he had always been hidden away in a corner, feeling guilty about wanting to kill his parents, about wanting to kill the world. He hid himself away and felt guilty about himself and I hid him away in a corner and felt guilty about his existence. When I realized that this hiding had been going on all my life I understood that hiding him had been one of the primary functions of my personality.

And so I apologized to him, I told him I was sorry he had felt the way he did, that his anger was understandable but that at that early time there was no way for him to understand. That he was angry because there was no one to hear him and help him understand what was happening in him, and that wishing to kill was the outlet of that great energy. But I also told him that he had not killed, in fact his wish to kill had become in me the seed that had led me to go out and try to heal, and it had led me to try to help parents be kinder and more understanding with their children. I told him that it had become the direction of my entire life.

He said, "Wow, you mean all of that came out of me?"

I said, "Yes!"

As I lay in the bed with the little black boy in my arms I felt an energy current running through my body, and every circuit in my body fully energized by this current. My body writhed and old frozen twists in my body began to undo themselves, from the inside. Old frozen muscles began to melt. Old twists and turns in my personality and relationships began to make sense. The entire room was filled with a golden glow and I began to feel whole, I lay there for over two hours exulting in this experience. I knew I had come home.

That little black boy was a seed in me, and out of him grew the person I have become, so I am deeply thankful to him, but I also feel the isolation in which he has lived his entire life, the aloneness that could never seem to be quenched, the unwillingness to enter into the social dimension of life.

I embraced him and hold him even now, and I will hold him for the rest of our lives. He was powerful and valiant. He took on the whole world—and we won.

CHAPTER 29

ENCOUNTERS WITH MOTHER

I am at a training in Austria. I am being guided on a journey by another member of the group. The journey shocks me. My guide is Mother Earth. She receives me into her arms in the most loving manner and I feel truly and lovingly held. She tells me that she has always held me and that she always will. I feel so deeply comforted.

Then she tells me that I should not go to Portugal the following week, as I had planned, in fact I have already purchased my plane ticket and reserved a rental car, so I am stunned by her telling me this and I don't say a word about it to my human guide. I think of several ways to get around it: maybe Mother Earth will have another suggestion before I am to leave on the flight, maybe the airline will cancel the flight to Portugal, etc.

Mother Earth is very specific about what I should do instead. "I will guide you to a place in the Burgenland," she says. I have been interested in helping found a community in Austria and the Burgenland is one of the regions where land is affordable. But for years I have also been wanting to go to Portugal and am seriously intending to go there.

So the journey throws me into severe conflict.

That same night I have the following dream: I had purchased an older Volkswagen. I was at a mechanics shop, not that I had intended to be there but somehow I ended up there. I was going over the cars needs and there was a young brash kid there who seemed to have some schemes for the car. I had the feeling he was going to install used parts and charge me for new ones or something similar. I didn't trust him. I saw the underside of the car and saw that it had no tailpipe from the muffler on back. I was making a list of everything it needed. I had been encountered by a man earlier who was talking to me about a particular garage that I had been to once.

Awakening from the dream and as I continue to hold it in my awareness throughout the day I recognize that I am much like the weaselly kid, and that I have been trying to weasel out of doing what Mother Earth told me to do; feeling the conflict but not confronting it directly, thinking it will resolve itself, or that something will happen that will decide it for me, but not just taking a strong stance myself, one way or another. I see this as a pattern in my life.

The other realization that comes to me is the way my own mother was so intrusive in decisions I had made. If I decided something with which she disagreed she was relentless in trying to persuade me that I should decide differently, along the lines of her own thinking. Eventually I came to say very little, if she asked something, I would not know until I knew what her decision was so I could decide along those lines. I gave up expressing my own desires in order to reduce the conflict.

I have lived my life with a film of mother around me, unable, or unwilling, to interact directly with my world. No wonder I have focused on experience! I am even unable to write just for myself, but always feel as if I am writing for an audience that would include my mother and her censorship of my own fucking will and desires!

The next morning in the training group I am leading, when I hold the talking staff I tell the group about my journey and also about what Mother Earth has told me, also saying that it threw me into such conflict that I did not even tell my human guide.

I also tell the group about my dream, it has happened the night before the training ends and we only have half a day remaining, but Horst offers to guide me. I ask inside and am told that I should journey with the dream. After serious consideration I tell the group about this and I lay down in the center of the group. Stefanie scribes the journey for me.

As I lay in the center of the group I call out for a guide to the dream. A cartoon figure of a short little French detective with a pencil line of a mustache, brash and direct, appears. I ask if he is my guide. "Ab-so-lootly," he replies in English with a French accent. "Come weez me!"

He leads me back to the garage where the Volkswagen is. He walks around it. "Eet ees quite an automobile!", he says and asks, "How many peeple can feet eento a Volkswagen?" I don't know the answer to the obvious joke he is asking and I tell him so. "Two hundred meelion," he replies. I laugh at his excessiveness.

I ask him what needs to happen here. I feel a great pain in my heart. He removes a stethoscope from his jacket and listens to my heart. "Beeg problems een heart. Beeg hurts een heart." I become aware of a big hurt in my heart. He listens again to my heart. "You have a Volkswagen een your heart," he says in surprise. "Thees Volkswagen ees full of two hundred meelion peeple. Zat ees too many!" I laugh at his audacious sense of humor.

He reaches up into my heart and opens the backdoor of the VW that is there. A stream of people begin pouring out. I am surprised because each person is dressed formally in black. I am suddenly back at my grandfather's funeral. I was four years old when he was killed in a strange accident. He had gone to Belen in his Ford model A coupe to purchase a block of ice for the small store that he ran. The block of ice weighed three hundred pounds and was placed in the trunk of his little car. On the way back to Los Lunas, coming down a steep slope a boy with a cow and a calf were walking along the side of the road. As my grandfather approached the calf began to wander into the road. My grandfather stepped on the brakes, the block of ice slid forward, crashed through the cab of the car, slammed into his head and broke his neck. The car overturned.

My grandfather was taken by ambulance to the hospital in Albuquerque where he lived, paralyzed, for nine more days before he died.

The family was torn apart by this loss. My grandfather, Jesus Gallegos, was a very large man in many ways. He was sheriff of Valencia County. He ran a small store and a garage, he had rental property and a large apple orchard as well as the family home in which many of his thirteen children were born. My father, Eligio, was the oldest.

His death was sudden and unexpected and a strange set of circumstances emerged from the death that was to change the life of the Gallegos family from that time on. My grandfather, in spite of being a prominent businessman in town, was not financially liquid and so had borrowed twelve hundred dollars from the doctor who lived across the street from him, Dr. Witwer, in order to finance his current political campaign. Being sheriff in Valencia

County was an elected office which my grandfather had held for a number of years. Upon his death Dr. Witwer informed the family that he needed to be repaid the twelve hundred dollars for which he held a signed note. The story that came down to me was that Grandpa Jesus's children agreed to hold an auction within the family, to auction off my grandfather's holdings, in order to pay the debt that he had incurred from Dr. Witwer. It is obvious that my grandmother should have inherited all of my grandfather's property and could easily have sold a small portion of it in order to pay off the debt since the property was otherwise free and clear of any indebtedness.

Prior to the auction my uncle, Celedon, who was married to my father's sister, Teresa, came to my father and suggested that he not enter the auction but that Celedon would enter a bid for my father since the property should rightfully be his as the eldest son. My father thought this a good idea, God knows why. My mother was deeply suspicious of such an offer and tried to talk my father out of it but he was adamant.

The evening of the auction my father stayed home, waiting for Celedon to come by and give him the deed to the property in exchange for whatever the bid had been. I have memories of that evening. It got darker and darker, my mother began to worry and my father assured her that Celedon would come by at any time, that he was completely trustworthy. But as the evening wore on and it got later and later my father finally got in his model A Ford and drove the mile into town. He returned some hours later with blood in his eye, ready to kill. Celedon had entered the only bid, twelve hundred dollars, and immediately signed over the property to his neighbor Antonio Archuleta, a local barber, for the amount of the bid.

His story to my father was that there was such strife among the children that it was better to take the property completely out of the family so that the family could be in harmony. I remember my mother trying to calm my father down, he had come home to get his gun, and saying to him that we had not lost anything since the property had not belonged to us in the first place, that we still had our home, and that it would not be worth going to jail for such a deed, that the property was already in the hands of Antonio Archuleta and killing Celedon would not bring it back. It was a frantic and disquieting evening and there were elements in it that a four year old did not understand.

I am four years old at the funeral. I am a sponge for all the feelings that are there and I don't understand what is going on. Feelings of loss, of anger, of sadness, of perplexity, of shock and blankness. My grandmother's obvious grief—Plains Indian women would sometimes cut off a little finger in order to make the pain more tangible when they had lost a mate in battle, but her tribal heritage was either Pueblo or Apache.

I feel quite frantic, not knowing what to do with all of these feelings, and I seek out my mother for comfort. As people prepare to go to the burial my mother sends me off with my aunt to play with the other children and assures me that she will just be in the next room. After a few minutes of playing half-heartedly I seek to return to my mother and am informed that she has left but that she will be back very soon. I become livid, I have been lied to, I need my mother and she isn't there. All the conflicting feelings I have had until now pour into this rage and I want to smash everything!

The Frenchman suddenly says, "Only one hundred meelion to go!" as people are pouring out of the VW all dressed in formal black. "It hurts," I say to him. "Oui," he replies, "Volkswagens are heavy!"

The final person climbs out of the VW and I am glad it is over but the Frenchman then walks over to the other side, reaches for the door on that side and says, "Ready?" He waits until I stop laughing and then yanks the door open.

Women pour out of this side, only women. I realize that any time a woman is in pain I feel a need to help her. And I am suddenly a child with my grandmother Martina. She really loved me. There was no way I needed to qualify for her love as I did with my parents. After she moved to a small adobe house in town that seemed to have escaped the auction I stayed with her many nights so she wouldn't be alone. She was a wonderful woman, non-judging, and always with a sparkle in her eye. I only now recognize who she was in that community, and how people would come visit her. She always had a pot of beans cooking on the stove, and some red chile, and fresh tortillas, from morning until night. Whoever would come to her door would be invited in to sit at the table and eat. She would serve them. And if we stopped by to visit and did not eat she would prepare some food for us to take home. I suddenly understand what a big part of my early life this woman was. I see beyond Grandma to her larger spirit and I realize that I carry a large part of her in my own deeper being.

She accepted me for who I was without judging me. "Don Estevan" she used to call me even when I was just a small boy. I did not understand until now what a kind and loving anchor she had been for me in a cluttered world, nor how much of her I still carry in myself. When I was a professor in Georgia I went to visit her at the nursing home in Albuquerque. She was bedridden and unable to walk. With the same sparkle in her eye that had always been there, she said to me in Spanish: "I am ninety-nine years old. Why doesn't He come and get me? Doesn't He know I'm ready to go? This poor old body is all worn out, it can't even get around anymore, why doesn't He come and get me?"

I had intended to return the next summer with a tape recorder and record stories of her early life in New Mexico. She was half Indian and had lived through the most amazing time of change in the world. She could neither read nor write. But she had a memory that was keen and precise and I wanted to write a book about her life. But He came to get her before I could return.

I'm back at the VW now. Women are still pouring out of it. Still a few more to go. All women, wearing colorful dresses. I watch them stepping out of the VW in my heart, being helped graciously by the Frenchman. I recognize how much responsibility I felt I needed to take for these women.

Memories and thoughts about my own mother rush forth. Following the loss of my grandfather's estate she realized she would have to be responsible for supporting our family. She had originally thought that she would stay at home, writing, painting, taking care of her children, and being part of that larger family in the little community of Los Lunas. But with my grandfather gone, and my father having only a third grade education, she returned to teaching.

However, there was no teaching job available in Los Lunas so she and I and my older sister, Juliet, moved to Nambé Pueblo, ninety miles to the North and she taught the third grade. She was nicknamed Coy because of her natural shyness but she put on a tough front and became active in education for the rest of her life. The Katherine Powers Gallegos grade school in Los Lunas was named for her a few years before her death. While we were in Nambé my father had remained in Los Lunas working for the Huning Mercantile Company twelve hours a day, six days a week for fifty dollars a month. My sister, Rosalie, commented years later after he had died how difficult it must have been for him to have remained in Los Lunas for the rest of his life after what he had done. My mother taught in Albuquerque for two more years before she could finally get a teaching job in Los Lunas and we moved back to our little adobe house that my father had built.

I remember her many comments about how difficult it was for a woman to advance professionally in this world that was run by men. Although she never mentioned it as such it was obvious that she felt she should have advanced to the position of super-intendent of schools but that she never would because she was a woman. She did ultimately design her own position of school supervisor, a position that was responsible for obtaining funding from various available federal programs for the school system. She was the first anglo woman to marry a hispanic man in that com-munity and came to be very loved, ultimately having taught most of the people who lived there, and it was their spontaneous deci-sion to name the school after her. I recognize how much of her world view is embedded in me as the Frenchman helps her out of the VW.

He reaches in with his umbrella and pokes around.

"Any more to come out?", he asks. No one answers.

"Now we have to drive the car out," he announces turning to me. "Do you like to drive?"

I answer that I do. "Me too!", he says as he climbs into the driver's seat.

I am in the passenger's seat as he revs the engine.

"Ready?", he asks. He then shoves it into gear and races down a ramp that leads out of my heart—directly into a lake! We scramble out of the VW and swim to shore as the car sinks.

"Zat was good!" , he says, satisfied. "Zat ees where zee Volkswagen belongs."

I ask if anything more needs to happen. "No. See you later," he yells as he hops on a bicycle and peddles away.

I wave at him and say, "Thank you!" My heart is unbelievably lighter. A fresh breeze is blowing through it. I had no idea how much of other people I was carrying in it.

The weeklong training ends and I go to Munich where I spend the night at my friend Bianca's apartment, still very much in conflict about whether to go to Austria as Mother Earth had told me or to Portugal as I had originally planned. I tell her the situation and she offers to guide me on a journey to seek the answer.

As I relax and call out for a guide Mother Earth is again holding me. I ask her what I should do and she answers that I know very well what I should do. I ask several other questions and she informs me that I already know, and I do. The next morning, borrowing Bianca's car, I head for Austria and the Burgenland.

As I drive I am in a deeply feeling state, and I have the strange sensation that as a child there was an encounter with my mother that was an encounter of power, and that it left me in a state of shock, numbed, not being fully present. That feeling stays with me and there are vague memories of something happening when I was a small boy that was very unusual in my interactions with my mother. Something like a situation where she just took over my mind, like deep hypnosis or deep conditioning, resulting from a state of shock which left me obedient but blank.

I drive around Austria. It is like a country that was set down in a park. I am overwhelmed by the beauty of the mountains and the forests. I drive aimlessly, allowing myself to be guided by pure feel rather than by anything logical other than the need to find shelter for the night and to be aware of others driving on the same highway.

Along the way I have flashes of memories and visions. In one of them my mother is a kind of wispy fabric or membrane that slips between me and any situation that confronts me, she is essentially my interface with the world.

I see her running across the street when I was a boy. I had bought a comic book in a drug store in Albuquerque. As I am returning to the car another boy stops me and asks to see the comic book I had bought. I hand it to him and he grabs it and runs away. My mother, who has been waiting in the car, leaps out and runs the boy down, yelling at him and making him give the comic book back. I feel some concern for the boy, compassion for him. I see how she was trying to protect me from the harsh realities of the world and I also see what a strong controlling dimension she had. Memory after memory runs through me.

Upon returning from Austria to Germany to begin the training there I attempt to rewrite what I have just written above. I am going to change some of what I said about mother being a film or membrane around me but something goes haywire with the computer, it crashes and freezes and the line about my mother being a film around me appears twice and underlined! I cannot move on and must restart the computer. It is obvious the Universe is trying to tell me something.

I realize that I must go more deeply into this membrane that envelops me. I feel encased by it. Although I can see through it what I see is distorted. When I try to do something my actions are somehow dampened, mushy. Ineffective. It feels like a pink rubber membrane that keeps me from seeing the world directly, in its pure rawness. And in order for me to interact fully with the world my actions must pass through the membrane, yet they do not, the membrane holds me back, as if it were rubber or elastic. Moving through the membrane requires tremendous effort and it is easier to remain passive.

I go to a gym to exercise, aware that I am encased in this rubber membrane like a sausage. The membrane seems to limit my awareness to my immediate surface. As I am standing in one of the exercise machines, supported by my elbows, a machine for strengthening my gut by bringing my legs forward, I suddenly have the feeling that the membrane is beginning to tear, to split, to rip open from my head on down. I emerge forth from this encasement with the memory that I was born with a veil. This must be how birth must feel. I am shoved forth into a world where I am totally unprotected, the air is cool and raw, and my awareness suddenly fills the room. I also feel very faint, like I will pass out, and thoughts of heart attacks come to me. I realize what a fear I have of this new place, a place where I am not protected by my mother and where my own interactions with the world are direct and have consequences. But I also feel free and fresh and present in my life.

Later that week, at the training in Germany I am working with a group of women. We are in the second year of training, halfway through it, and as we gather for the second week of the training I have the feeling that we should work with dreams. That night I have several dreams:

I have difficulty holding onto the first dream, as if I am still in it. There were two people, a man and a woman, and as the man woke he discovered a black widow spider's nest behind his ear. I either woke up or the dream continued and I or someone else squashed the black widow spider.

Second dream: I was in a class. A woman in the class did good work and was a favorite of the teacher's. He never said much to me even though my work was just as good and just as fast. Then she and I were in a red VW van. I was driving. I stepped on the brakes only to discover that there were virtually none at all so I drove between two lanes of cars that were stopped ahead of me and just beginning to move. Eventually we reached a side place where I could let the van come to a stop as I down shifted.

Then we found ourselves in another class. Every person in that class had a computer and on the screen of the computer was a corpse. The corpse needed to be prepared in some way in order to begin the class and the woman knew how to do that.

When my training group meets the following morning we split up into groups of three and I journey into these dreams. I call out for a dream guide and I see a swan swimming on a pond. The swan is alternately black and white. I think that perhaps there are two swans but there is in fact only one. I have difficulty seeing it because it is shifting back and forth between black and white. I ask if it is my dream guide and it says that it is. It says it will take me into the dreams all at once, into all parts of both dreams at the same time.

My thinking realizes that it can only pursue the events in a linear fashion, one happening after another, and that it is helpless when everything happens at once. My thinking realizes that it cannot follow and that it must remain behind while my experience ensues, I must wait before I can say a word. The experience is simultaneous and intense and I can only describe it later. I plunge myself into the experience.

Following the experience I reconstitute the event verbally as best I can:

The white part of the swan heads over to the first dream and seems to balance the blackness of the black widow spider. The black part of the swan heads over to the three parts of the second dream. I realize that the corpse in the computer was me. I was also the black widow spider that was squashed long ago. At that time I split into a feminine and a masculine side in order to avoid punishment, because the punishment was always less for one part then for the other, depending on what situation I was in. Also, one of them was also deemed worthier than the other.

I was also the vehicle in which these two parts were riding and have had to travel in between all the stalled others, through the red light, and finally was able to come to rest on the side of the main highway.

As I am going through this experience there is a flood of energy into my body. My thinking can no longer keep it out. To my thinking my body was dangerous. It was the source of pain because it was always beaten whenever it would not do what it was told to do by father, by mother, by teachers. My aliveness was squashed like the spider. Only the computer remained. One part of me was dead, the other alive. One part feminine, the other part masculine. My body waited a long, long time for me to wake up. I was only fully alive in my dreams. My body was gradually frozen away from my thinking because my thinking was always afraid that my body would be beaten if it did something that was not allowed. My thinking tried to protect me in this way but at a great sacrifice. However, as far as my thinking knew, this was the only way I would survive. My thinking was afraid of my aliveness, but one cannot live from thinking alone.

The tearing of my body into parts was done by me in order to protect myself. Aliveness was always there, unified, but its unity died. Only the computer survived. I could not allow aliveness to be free. It was too dangerous. The feelings that have always been there were not just feelings, that was my body's aliveness! To my thinking it was only feeling; to my body it is the very aliveness itself. To disallow feeling is to disallow aliveness. I know what it is like to be imprisoned!

During this journey into my dreams my body is becoming more and more alive. My body heaves, great groans emerge, my ribcage squeezes the very last breath out of me, my legs churn in the air, my back arches itself. Life is now flowing through the pain that has always been there in my buttocks and back. I feel alive and limber and centered down in my belly rather than in my head.

The swan asks that I become it. I merge myself into it. I feel that inside it is both black and white, down to the very seed-kernel that it is. I feel how peaceful it is and how it flows so effortlessly and trustingly over the water, trusting that the water will always support him. I experience its two broad feet giving it direction under the water, taking him wherever he wants to go.

He can also fly when he wishes to on his strong wings, or he can go onto land to his nest. He is very still inside, very peaceful and awake. I see a graveyard and am aware that in German it is not called a graveyard but a peace yard (Friedhof). We don't know what freedom is, only burial. I experience how peace is not being buried inside. My entire body was frozen for such a long time.

But I am now the swan, fully alive without needing to do a thing outwardly. The stream of aliveness flows through him. Life is one, it is not separate, nor should it be.

Swan tells me I should emerge from him but very slowly. I emerge slowly, and my head is the last of me to emerge. I am a living spirit and I see Steve's body lying on the bank in the grass, deeply at peace. I go there very slowly and feel how beautiful the meadow is, how lovely the sky, the day, the lake with the swan. There is a river that runs into the lake. There is a forest on the hill. The forest sees all that happens. Trees are immensely old beings, and have seen everything. They are ancient and noble, and they see everything.

As this living spirit I ask the forest if I cannot better be a tree. The forest answers in German, "You can, of course." I feel how deeply I have always loved these trees. I feel how the earth's love flows through the trees, first into the roots, then through the strong trunk and out into the numerous branches and then through the leaves back into the sky. Then I experience how the sun sends its love, through the leaves, into the branches, through the trunk and roots back into the earth. It is through the trees that the sun and the earth love one another. I see how whenever a human cuts a tree down some of this love is cut away.

We don't realize what we do! If this love ever dies, we will all die! I know now what I must write! I feel it deep in my belly! People have become so dead! I can let my aliveness flow into books. Books are a little part of these trees; the trees have sacrificed themselves so that people may find their way back into their own aliveness. I say to the trees, "I know now why I am alive and what I must do." They answer, "Yes!" Then my living spirit, sorry to be leaving them, flows back to Steve's body lying in the meadow, embraces him gently and tenderly, flowing into him but also remaining around him like silver water. Steve's body sits up and communes with the trees. They are deeply happy. They have sacrificed themselves so for mankind. They don't want to be slaughtered anymore, so disrespectfully, without us even knowing what we do.

CHAPTER 30

THE TWIN TOWERS

The first edition of this book was almost ready to go to press when the hideous events involving the destruction of theWorld Trade Center occurred on September 11, 2001.

Because of the enormity of this event and its impact on me and on the world I have elected to include the following three journeys. But before I describe the journeys I must first speak about the perspective of the terrorist.

We live in a world that has come more and more to be conveyed in words and concepts. We have not matured to the point where we are able to stand outside of those concepts and experience the world, ourselves included, as an ongoing miraculous living experience. Many people carry around grievous injuries that never get addressed in any way. And the personality becomes frozen around those injuries with the perspective of preventing further injury, but also with the stance of always being focussed on the source of the injury. The original injury or injuries may be hidden under many layers of just such protective coatings. This provides the template for a serious polarization of one's view of the world.

Living only at the level of that great gift, language and thinking, language being the toolbox of thinking, brings it to the level of no longer being a gift but a cage. To place God only at the level of conceptualization, where the concept is subject to the twin terrors of polarization and generalization, is to limit reality and God to the structure of thought. The experience of tremendous division is the result. To be destructive while claiming an alliance with God does not make the destruction an act of God. It is still the act of a divided mind with a false allegiance.

We must go deeper than thought. We must enter our own being to that point where we directly experience our own alignment with the Universe. And if the alignment is not there, if it has been covered over by injury and protection, then we must forge our way even more deeply. This is the beauty of the path of deep imagery: it allows our path and our alignment with the universe to deepen and deepen, carrying us through the injuries and allowing their healing.

The stance of the terrorists, that they will kill thousands of people whom they have never met for the love of God or Allah has unfortunately been too often repeated during our short history. It was a view held by the Roman Catholic Church during the Inquisition, it was maintained by Hitler during his political reign (only he was focussed on a master race rather than on God), it is the stance of many fundamentalists in many religions: the perspective of loving God but hating people (or hating only certain people). I have also seen the same polarity in reverse: hating God (for the type of world he has created) but loving people. The problem is one of an inner division that gets overly heated to the point of coloring one's entire view of existence.

There has also been such a tendency in the past few thousand years to politicize life to the point that wherever one is born or lives there is an overarching political organization that assumes the right to impose (or require) a particular way of thinking and acting. We in the United States have come through a period of political history where we were taught that Communists were anathema and we in our Democracy (or Capitalocracy) were fine people.

Few people today are nurtured to grow into their own true wholeness, yet each person contains the seed of that orientation. The more divided a person is the more insistent the call toward wholeness. Unfortunately many of the philosophies that are espoused today portray that wholeness as only attainable after death. Yet it is fully available now and is a definite part of the inherent natural direction in our present lifetimes.

Many maps are available that portray a world that is divided in two with no passageway for healing or growing that world into a single wholeness within oneself. Unfortunately such maps also place wholeness (or holiness) at one end of a polarity, not recognizing the inherent illogic of such a stance. True wholeness cannot be divided. You cannot arrive at wholeness by destroying its opposite. Wholeness is only achieved by embracing the opposites and allowing the unitive transformation to take place. We humans are the creators of division and we can only heal it individually within ourselves.

I had arrived in Austria on September 10 to conduct a training and on the afternoon of the second day of the training the large group had split up into smaller groups of three people each. One of the two people I was with had just completed a journey when Horst entered, apologized for intruding, and told us the news. It was only a few hours since the attacks in New York had happened and we rushed immediately to the only TV set in the building. The newscaster showed clips from CNN of the two passenger planes, one after the other, slamming into the two towers of the World Trade Center in New York, the panic on the streets, and ultimately the giant dust cloud as the second tower sank to the ground. I had difficulty grasping the enormity of the event. On the one hand it seemed impossible and on the other hand it looked like something out of a movie. We spent the evening glued to the TV set which had continuous coverage on one of its two channels.

For the remaining days of the training we held a moment of silence both morning and evening, each in our own way focussing on healing for the victims and wishes for a positive outcome rather than blind retaliation. These moments of silence had been proposed spontaneously by members of the group.

On the morning following the attack each member of the training group spoke about how the event had affected them. We then separated into smaller groups of three and went to different rooms to do our journeys for the day.

One of the ways I have come to deal with events that are irreparable is to ask if the energy of the event may in some way grow me, so that in that way at least something positive comes out of the disaster. That is what I did on this occasion.

CHAPTER 31

THE SNAKE

Andrea was guiding me. After a beautiful relaxation she asked me to approach the place where my imagery happens. For me it has always been a giant wooden door, deeply carved, very ancient. It is so immense that it need open only a tiny crack for me to scurry through. On the other side is a jungle full of animals.

On this particular occasion, strangely enough, rather than appearing in my own bodily form I appear as a raccoon. As I go through the door into the jungle I call out and ask if there is any animal available to guide me to a place of using the energy of the previous days events for my own growing.

Immediately a giant snake appears. I initially think it is going to devour me, since I am a raccoon, and the snake says that it knows my thoughts and that it could devour me if it wished, but instead it invites me to follow it. It moves through the jungle at a tremendous pace, like a train, and I have to run just to stay close behind it. It says that I can ride it if I wish and it then reaches under me with its tail and flips me up onto its back. It is such a large snake that I have to stretch my arms out wide in order to cling to it.

It flies through the air and takes me directly to the two burning towers of the World Trade Center. Snake says, "Do you see? Life can come to an end quite suddenly. But life is also quite powerful and tenacious. People don't treasure life enough, until they begin to lose it."

As I look I see that life is remarkably light and fluid, but that it is also extremely strong. It is more fluid than light and yet powerful like water that wears away stone. I tell snake that I still cannot fully grasp the destruction of the two towers. Snake replies that no one can fully grasp it. I then see the Pentagon burning, the airplane and the passengers not knowing what is going on, and the plane that crashed near Pittsburgh.

Then we are up in the air once again. Snake says, "The greater the imbalance, the greater must be the impact to come back into balance." As I look below I see tribal people in Africa who only wish to live in balance with nature.

I ask snake, "How can I use the energy of this incident for my own growing?" Snake answers, "You can use it to bring yourself more into balance." "How can that happen?" I ask.

Without answering snake immediately begins to fly faster and faster. I am clinging to snake for my very life. Snake leaves the realm of the earth, flies beyond the solar system, out beyond the galaxy and further still. Snake is flying so fast that I cannot see where we are, I see only a blur of color and fleeting shapes that I cannot distinguish. I suddenly become aware that I have lost all reference points. The earth is not available as a reference system and I recognize nothing at all as we stream out into the universe. I don't know where I am nor how far we have gone. I grasp the snake even tighter and realize that now I only have this snake as my reference point. It is all that I know out here.

Snake says to me, "You only have me as a reference point and I am your own energy!"

I suddenly see that as I was growing up I was taught to take everything else as a reference point but never my own energy! Everything else had some value but never me! I see the plane crashing into the tower. Snake says, "All the reference points you learned in your life have now disappeared! Feel my energy as a part of the Universe. This part is always in contact with all the other parts of the universe, there is no separation!"

I see that I have always been in touch with this part but that my awareness was glued to everything else but this. That was the separation! I ask snake what it needs from me and he replies he needs for me to love him.

I immediately feel fear. I realize there was always fear of loving the snake, sometimes overwhelming fear. I see an immense history of people being taught to fear the snake. I see the bible: there is a tremendous fear of loving the snake. But then I see that you can never love another person fully until you have loved your own snake, for everyone has a snake!

"That is the separation. Your inability to love me!"

I become fully aware that the snake that I had so feared had always been in the right side of my body!

We are now back in New York over the destroyed World Trade Center, smoke is billowing up. Snake says, "Because people fear the snake instead of loving it, it gets loose and is very destructive!"

I then experience that there are in fact two snakes: one in my left side that is very fearful and the one in my right side that is very powerful. I realize that I have always identified with the snake on the left side and that I have been terrified of the snake on the right side. I then realize that the fear on the left side is also love! When it pulls back and retreats it is fear, but when it goes forward it is love.

Both snakes then rise up in me and meet deliberately face to face in the middle of my forehead. This powerful meeting vibrates throughout my body and it comes to full focus right in the center of my forehead. I recognize this animal! It is the Sisiutl from Mexican symbology: the single snake with two heads. It embraces the universe and comes back to meet itself face to face. I realize Sisiutl is both the symbol and the energy of wholeness.

CHAPTER 32

GRANDPA JESUS

The following day I am guided on another journey, this time by Traude. When I call out for an animal a Lynx appears. I am overjoyed. I haven't seen Lynx in many years. When I say hello to him he turns into a cat, but also with pointed ears. He starts up some stairs and bids me to follow.

We enter a house or a building. It is one of the buildings of the World Trade Center and I follow him. I have two simultaneous experiences: one is that I am entering the World Trade Center the way it was before the destruction, and the other experience is that we are entering it following its destruction.

I ask the cat about that. "Which one is the real World Trade Center?" Cat looks at me and asks: which one is the real Steve? As I look closely I see an image of me and also a Steve that has no form, just a bundle of experiences right now. And as I look back at the cat it also has no form, it is also only a bundle of experiences.

I immediately hear the words from the Diamond Sutra: Emptiness is Form, Form is none other than Emptiness. And I can see and feel that feelings are only fluid unless we hang onto them and freeze them.

And the nature of Being is to be fluid. I hear the Buddha saying to not cling but to let go. It is totally related to feelings; not clinging to a form. Then I look at myself: where am I clinging or freezing my emotions?

I feel a discomfort in the right side of the back of my neck. As a child I used to be seized by a sudden pain right there, especially when around my father, as if the muscle would spontaneously contract and my head would jerk backward, seeming to happen in order to protect me, to pull me back away from him in order not to be hit, like an old form of frozen protection. I focus into that place in my neck and all I see is a frozen ice cube, really hard and cold.

I suddenly remember that my grandfather was killed by a block of ice that had slid forward in the bed of his car and struck him in the back of the head, breaking his neck. My grandfather's death changed our family completely, changed his family totally, and even changed the nature of the town of Los Lunas. And it feels like I carry the burden of these changes in the back of my neck!

I then see my grandfather. I have never seen him before in any of my journeys. I feel sorry that he died. He looks at me warmly. He was always warm and friendly toward me when I was a child. I suddenly realize that he had great hopes for me in the family. He felt that I would be one of the mainstays. He didn't know that he would die so soon. My mother loved him and thought highly of him. His wife, my grandmother, was heartbroken at his death. It tore the whole family apart. He would have been a strong support for me had he lived. I am aware suddenly that I had no grandpa to grow up with. What a difference it would have made in my life. He would have greatly softened the severity of my father. I say to him, "I'm sorry that you died."

He replies, "Yes, but it is good to see you now. And you are successful. You went on your path that you might not have taken if I had lived."

I feel what a strong person he would have been in my life. He says, "I can still be a strong person in your life."

I ask, "How can this happen?"

He replies, "Let me support you."

I see him holding me in his arms as a small boy. I see how he cared for me more than my father ever did. I can feel his warmth and his strength as he holds me. He asks, "Are you willing to be held by me?"

"Yes!" I feel warm, big, strong.

I realize how brittle I have been; acting as if his death were the end of our relationship. It wasn't. It doesn't need to be. I rub the back of my neck. I had no grown up man I could turn to as I grew up. But he is in that place now. I feel the continuity of the family that I didn't get from my father.

He stands behind me, behind the place on my right side where the contraction was in my neck. And thenI see my grandmother standing beside him, supporting my left side from behind. They are both standing behind me and supporting me. I recognize how much they cared for me.

I feel the cat rubbing against my leg. It is time to go. Both of my grandparents are standing behind me, supporting me, caring for me. I had never felt any support from behind before now. Now I feel not only support but the continuity of being linked to the human race. The cat is now a kitten, playfully biting my fingers, and I thank her for bringing me here.

CHAPTER 33

THE INVISIBLE ROOM

Twelve days later I am in Germany in the Allgau region conducting a training. On the first day of the training I am part of a triad consisting of Angela and Robert. Robert has elected to journey into issues having to do with father and Angela has elected to journey to issues around mother. I have no idea what I will journey to as I don't sense any agendas. When it is my turn to journey Angela is my guide and Robert scribes my journey.

I am deeply relaxed through Angela's guiding and I approach the great carved wooden door through which I go in order to meet my animals. I call out for any animal that wishes to come and the eagle from my forehead comes immediately, swoops down, takes the collar of my shirt in its beak and carries me away.

I ask where he is taking me and without opening his mouth he answers that were he to answer me he would drop me. He carries me over the ocean and over a continent that is studded with jungles and deserts. Then I see a large hotel below. A portico leads into it and the eagle flies me directly into the lobby and sets me down. I notice immediately that all of the employees are animals. There is a crocodile behind the reception desk. He welcomes me and tells me that my room is ready. A platypus who is the porter takes my bags although I was not aware that I had any bags. I look to Eagle to see if he is coming as well and he informs me that he will return for me when I am ready.

The platypus takes my bags into the elevator and I follow. He closes the door and we ascend, going quite high. Eventually the elevator stops, the door opens, and I step directly into a curious room. The room is completely transparent yet I can see that it is a large hotel room. The platypus deposits my bags and wishes me a good stay, then he leaves. I look around in wonder. The walls are transparent and seem like elaborate picture windows. The room is high above a beautiful beach and I can look far out over the ocean. I have no idea why I am here or what I am to do so I go over to the transparent bed and lie down. The bed is beautifully soft and deeply comfortable. I am suddenly quite tired so I close my eyes and go to sleep and I immediately have a dream.

I find myself in a time long, long ago. I am standing before a large cave. To one side of the entrance and leaning against the earth mountain is a young man who wears a curious crown made of some deep blue substance that is unfamiliar to me. He is relaxed and I approach him and ask where I am. He looks at me and tells me that I am nowhere and everywhere.

His answer plunges me into the sudden recognition that I have always located myself in comparison to something else. Our maps are always measured and relative. Everything always exists in comparison to something else. I suddenly understand that the place of dreams, as the place of deep imagery, has no location the way aspects of our outer world are located. It just is where it is, without comparison.

I find myself shoved or drawn into a place deep within myself where I experience my existence as a given, without comparison and without requiring confirmation. I am stunned, for I recognize that this place has always been here, yet I traded it away long ago for confirmation of my existence from some other person or relative to some other object.

I look deeply into the young man's eyes and it is as if I am looking into eternity, into the very origins of being. Then suddenly I am the young man standing next to the entrance to the cave and people are coming by, looking at me and asking, "Who are you?"

I awake suddenly in the transparent room and know now where I am although I had never been in this room before. The Platypus enters and takes my bags. I stand up and follow him into the elevator and we are transported down to the lobby. In the lobby the crocodile at the desks says, "I hope you had a good stay, Sir." Eagle is there. He picks me up with his beak by the collar of my shirt and we fly back across the jungles and deserts, across the ocean, and to the place where we first met. As he sets me down he asks how my journey was. I answer, "Profound! Profound!" and hug him around the neck. I walk back through the large carved wooden door and as I do I realize that my imagery is always with me.

CHAPTER 34

INTO THE LIGHT

I call out for my animal of the eighth chakra. It is my whale but there is something different about it and I cannot quite tell what it is. It seems to have raised sides on it. It looks somewhat like a boat. It invites me to ride it and tells me it will take me on a journey. As I get on it I realize that it has white wings which it has never had before. It spreads its wings and flies me into the universe. I look around and am amazed at the color and the forms. I am awed by how large the universe is. It is vast and we are like a tiny speck of dust. And I wonder whether we will get lost.

A booming voice answers, "Everything is connected and everything is in its place."

I then realize that the notion of getting lost is just a human notion, and that from the standpoint of the universe there is no possibility of ever getting lost. I then ask, "But where do I belong?" The voice answers, "You have always been exactly where you belong." I reply, "But some of these places hurt!" The voice answers, "Pain also makes you walk your path." I ask the whale, "Where are we going now?"

There is no answer but everything is getting gradually brighter. I realize that the light is not only visual but that there is also a feeling to it, a feeling of warmth, like coming home. I suddenly realize that space is not empty, it is full of feelings. I feel deeply at home, there is no such thing as being lost. As it continues to get brighter I realize that being at home is being with the light.

I now see that there is a very bright light at the center of where we are flying to. Whale is flying directly toward this center, it is like coming home. I recognize that the whale has been there before. In the light everything is just one thing, there are no distinctions, all is one. As I merge more and more into the light I feel the places in my body that have to melt in order to merge with the light, that begin to free and release, It feels like a snake shedding its old skin. I hear a number of voices from the center of the light, gently urging me on, saying, "Come one, come on. Here he comes." They are young voices, gentle and encouraging.

I begin to wonder if I will ever be able to return once I enter the light fully. Suddenly the door of the room where I am journeying opens with a gust of wind and I am aware that I am journeying in this room.

A voice asks, "Where did he go?" Another answers, "He was called back. He'll visit us again at another time." I realize that the opening of the door was of as much consequence, and has as much weight as that center of light, and that I am to trust it equally.

The voices say, "Remember us." The whale says, "We have to go back." The whale, with a soft smile on its face, brings me back to the room. I thank it for the journey and it says, "We will go again some other time."

CHAPTER 35

THE FIRST SON

My relationship with my father is a theme that weaves itself through this book, through my injuries and healing journeys as it wove itself through my life. I was the only son of my parents' marriage. My relationship with my father was fraught with difficulty. For much of my life, I had no context into which to place his treatment of me. The journey I recount next was deeply healing for me in this regard.

A tiny Frog appears to me. He doesn't have much of a neck, his skin is colored with patches of greens. He reaches out and hugs me and feels how much I had to sacrifice in growing up. We understand each other without words. I'm deeply touched by his presence. I am aware of how deeply he feels, and also of how calm and enduring he is.

As we slowly sink to the bottom of the pond thoughts of my father come to me and of the way he lost no opportunity to shame me. His words to me more often than not spoke of shame: "You should be ashamed of yourself; aren't you ashamed of what other people might think of you? I'm ashamed to have a son like you." I feel how there was never any room for me to be with him.

I am then stunned by the frog's rejoinder: "You know you weren't his first son!"

Of course I knew! But for the first time in my life I see myself through my father's eyes in relationship to his first son and the understanding is startling!

When he was eighteen years old my father had fallen in love with a young woman from the village where he lived and she had borne him a son. My father was proud of his new son and wanted to marry his lover. However, my grandfather, having visions of establishing a political dynasty, wished to establish political connections through marriage in the old Spanish tradition, and objected to his eldest son marrying a woman of no repute. My father did not dare go against his father's wishes and his lover left the state with her new baby, aided financially by my grandfather.

Frog then asks me what would have happened if my father had married his young love and raised his first son. I realize the paradox I am in: if he had married her then he would never have married my mother and I would never have come along. The emotional detritus that I had to live through was part and parcel of my having a chance to come into this world at all!

I ask frog if anything else needs to happen on this journey.

Frog replies, "Isn't that enough?"

I feel as if something has been removed from the very marrow of my bones, something that was such a deep part of me that I have carried it as if it were who I am.

Frog sticks his tongue out at me and I thank him for bringing me here. He tells me to remain alone awhile, for I have just seen one of the foundations of my character.

HERON

After a while, I notice a Heron who says, "Hop up on my back." I do so and the heron suddenly transforms into a ladybug and flies away with me on her back. Her wings flutter at a tremendous rate and she flies this way and that and then lands in a pumpkin field. Pumpkins are lying strewn about and it feels like Halloween. I hop off of her back and ask her, "What needs to happen now?"

As it carries me I notice that it's very comfortable, quite cozy, as if I am being carried by a whirlwind of the universe. A voice suddenly says, "And why not?" Then I realize that everything that is happening is a movement of the universe, and that we are all parts of the universe. We think that we can get out of it but that is impossible, we can only go through it, and we need to know that we can only be exactly where we are, nowhere else. When I realize this a powerful energy, a great warmth, passes through my body, through my hands and feet.

Then I am suddenly an old Japanese monk sitting in meditation. The whirlwind is his breath. He is sitting there just experiencing his breathing, and feels a deep at home-ness. And as he sits in mediation suddenly many tiny green frogs flow through his imagination. Then they are gone. As he sits there he experiences his breathing as one of the primary movements of the universe. He feels completely trusting and centered in the universe. He feels what a great gift it is to be a part of the universe. There is no greater gift than to be a part of the universe.

As he sits there in meditation he feels the breath of the universe all around him. And he then experiences himself as the tiny green frog in balance with the universe, and when he breathes, the entire universe breathes through him.

Then the words come: "When I breathe the universe breathes, and when I sit, the universe sits." It's no big deal.

Then he suddenly stand up, stretches his hands into the sky—he is fat and happy—and says, "It's time for breakfast!" He looks just like the happy Buddha.

Then suddenly the tiny green frog jumps out of him onto the ladybug and they fly away toward the great wooden door. The frog hops off and the ladybug turns once again the grey heron. Frog and heron gassho to one another and frog goes through the great wooden door.

This journey healed much of my relationship with my father. Through it I came to appreciate how complex my presence had been for him. In many ways, I was a constant reminder of what he had lost: his first love and his first son. I am grateful that my path led me to understand the forces in his life that had impinged so impact-fully upon my own.

Yet the journey was also more than that. It brought home how deeply we need to appreciate all our aspects, all our experiences. It seems obvious that we should each appreciate the part of the universe that we are, regardless of whether we are frogs, herons, ladybugs, pumpkins, ghosts, or monks. We are all, equally, parts of the universe. Furthermore, the universe needs all of its parts in order to be completely whole, just as we do.

As we move into wholeness, we need every part that we are, even the tiniest, seemingly most insignificant part. This, after all, is the path to wholeness: the building of relationship with all our various alivenesses. My way of meeting these parts and thus moving more and more into wholeness has been to journey, that is, to work with the deep imagination.

CHAPTER 36

IMAGERY AS A PATH TO WHOLENESS

As I began this book by speaking about the confusion, terror, loneliness and hopelessness that engulfed my early life, and which motivated me to search for answers, let me end it by describing as best I can how I experience myself now and the world around me. My body is not an object, not even a biological specimen, but a magical dimension that has evolved over millions of years and that carries within itself the energies and knowledge of all of creation. It is a kind of doorway that allows me, whoever I may be, to come into the world always right now to act in whatever way the multitudes of powers in me formulate themselves into doing. I am both innocent of my acts and fully responsible for them; I inherently trust the goodness of their intention and am willing to be startled and amused by their own knowing. Many times I am not privy to that knowing until the event itself. I love the splendid creativity of the present moment.

I am fully comfortable with not knowing and I realize what a narrow domain "knowing" is. I spent most of my years of schooling hiding my not knowing behind the memorized thoughts and answers. "Not knowing" is an exciting place, adventurous, like a never ending landscape. Occasionally I have a feeling about or with someone else and a sense of puzzlement. I have learned that the feeling itself knows why it is there and if I just embrace that feeling and give it space within my own being, it eventually opens itself like a flower and shows me things that I had not known about the person and about myself.

People are treasure houses of creativity, and to spend time with a roomful of people, helping them come into a relationship with their deep imagery, is to be present with a roomful of living works of art in creation. It is thrilling.

The place of deep imagery within each of us is a place of deep original aliveness. Unfortunately we have come to treat it as a thing, somehow separate from us. Freud even called a part of it "the It" (das Es, which has been classically translated as "the Id"). We are separated from this place of deep original aliveness early in our childhood and spend much of our lives then searching for an anchor point in the world when it is there already, hidden deep within.

The place is kept hidden through the development of a tendency toward symbolization and interpretation. Whenever we are invited to journey deeper into our being we have a tendency to jump back into our thinking by interpreting, thus confounding the invitation, thinking we are fulfilling the invitation when we are actually avoiding it. We are afraid of leaving thought.

We feel that we must instill in children rules of behavior within society but those rules are already inherent in every child, and in a much more natural, organic way than our verbal laws. The child is born to be raised in a natural environment, including the presence of a loving tribal community. One or two people loving and nurturing the child is way too few.

The nuclear family is an injured fragment of a larger familiar whole, injured in the sense that it tries to sustain itself independent of the larger tribe. The child does not have the natural energetic pull from other caring adults in order to allow the fullness of its blossoming. Instead, in our present world, it must develop a protective callus around its being which, having happened much too early in the child's life, becomes a constriction of being rather than a support of being. We even have a name for this callus: the Ego.

Our society has become a social organization concerned with imposing patterns on growing children rather than supporting them in their own discovery. We treat them as if they were products going through an assembly line, trying to make them predictable and controllable, rather than exciting them about their natural creativity. We are systematically wasting the greatest natural resource there is, the whole human being.

The way back to wholeness is direct and simple, although it may be painful, and it could be accomplished globally in one generation. This would be a Manhattan Project worthy of who we are!

We must first recognize that we are the storytelling animals. We also need to know that all the stories we tell are just that: stories. No story is the equivalent of living. Yet most people today try to live a story instead of living their lives, and for this reason also, when their story goes wrong, many people take their lives.

One of the main stories we have learned is that the world is divided. We seldom learn that it is we who are divided. We are an incomplete being searching for completeness. We learned to abandon our completeness as a means of surviving in a synthetic environment where words and concepts have become more important than the reality that supports them.

Our way back into wholeness is simple: we must embrace in our awareness all of those dimensions of ourselves that we have seemingly lost. But this does not mean to act them out. Our awareness must stretch and grow to the point where it is capable of containing the multiplicity of energies that we in fact are. All of the polarities, complexities, confusions, conflicts, pains, joys, and qualities of greatness not yet developed are parts of our wholeness. But we must have a center around which these aspects can assemble.

If we have the mistaken understanding that our aliveness is already ripe then we think that all we need to do is to is to act, or to learn, or to accomplish. But if we acknowledge that our aliveness can always expand, grow, extend itself, either outward or inward, then we can be less complacent and recognize that one of our functions is to constantly accumulate aliveness.

One clear way to begin is by meeting with the council of the Chakra Animals. Their alignment and relationship with one another forms the nucleus of our wholeness. The embryo that we once were when in the womb did not stop growing; it kept accumulating and connecting greater and greater aspects of aliveness that had preceded humans, modifying them into new functions and gathering them together increasing their ability to interact and develop new relationships with the Universe. It was the ongoing unification of these various living capabilities which together then formed the child that you were born as.

But we need to recognize that our development does not end with our birth. It continues on, initially dependent upon the people that are around us and then becoming more and more dependent upon our own recognition and acceptance. The acceptance cannot take place haphazardly. It needs to proceed systematically. However we do not know the proper pace and sequence. Neither does our social milieu. The place where this is known is deep in the imagination, and it is through our development of a trusted ongoing communicative relationship that our aliveness, our awareness, and our maturity continue in their development. And just as our own aliveness originated out of that single mother-cell that was in our mother when she was born, we also need a center around which our continued growth and maturation can proceed. And this is the function of the aligned centers of aliveness that have been known since antiquity as 'chakras'.

As we embrace more and more of who we are we experience a deep and longed for healing. At points along the way these fractious dimensions jell suddenly into a new and larger being. This is the process that C. G. Jung referred to as transcendence.

Imagery is the most ancient living dimension of ourselves, and unfortunately, it is also one of the aspects that we learn early to abandon. Our relationship with deep imagery needs to be direct and simple: the reestablishing of a relationship that is respectful, where we are willing to be present, to communicate directly and immediately those thoughts, feelings, anticipations, expectations, hopes, fears, longings, loneliness, and love. And to listen in return. To open up a full and expressive dialogue with the deepest living part of who we are leads us back into our wholeness. Once we see it, it is so simple. And the alternative is so dangerous.

There is a positiveness and a natural goodness at the core of every human being. By journeying into our wholeness we reawaken and re-include this goodness. People are not naturally bad. It is buried injuries and inner divisions that cause people to do bad things.

Communication was intended to take place within ourselves as well as between people. That communication leads to a communion. And that communion leads us back into relationship with our fellow beings, the earth and nature, and the very Universe itself. We then experience our natural umbilication to the Universe.

I encourage you to begin your journey into wholeness today. Say hello to the deepest part of your imagination and allow room for a reply. The reply will occur in its own way which is perhaps not in the way that you expect. This will provide a good opportunity to look at the expectations you carry about your relationship to yourself! If you communicate what you are experiencing faithfully, and if you allow yourself to learn from your deepest living part, you will begin to change. It will be like a young shoot growing toward the light and recognizing that the roots are essential for its stability.

You are the only one who can make this journey. No one else can do it for you. Growing toward wholeness is a process that will continue your entire life. As each new day arrives there will be new opportunities for inclusiveness. Embrace them and relish the abundance of creation and the beautiful mystery of who you are. Being on the path of growing will itself bring a deep satisfaction, like making arrangements to visit the ultimate love.

This book is just my own attempt to indicate to you a possibility. Your journey will not be like mine although some of the directions may be similar. Allow room for the changes that will occur. The seed of who you are will remain constant but the blossoming will be endless. And then...tell the story that you need to tell.

I thank the Great Spirit of the Universe for the path
I have been given, every step of the way.

Eligio Stephen Gallegos
Embudo, New Mexico
January 23, 2018

194

REFERENCES

Gallegos, E. S. and Rennick, T. *Inner Journeys: Visualization in Growth and Therapy.* Turnstone Press, 1984. (currently out of print)

Gallegos, E. S. *The Personal Totem Pole: Animal Imagery, the Chakras, and Psychotherapy*, Moon BearPress, 1990.

Gallegos, E. S. *Animals of the Four Windows: Integrating Thinking, Sensing, Feeling, and Imagery.* Moon Bear Press, 1991.

Krishnamurti, J. *Commentaries on Living,* Third Series. Quest Books, 1960.

RESOURCES

FOR INFORMATION ON DEEP IMAGERY:

International Institute for Visualization Research
PO Box 632, Velarde NM 87582
www.deepimagery.net
www.facebook.com/deepimagery
IIVR@deepimagery.net

CONTACT THE AUTHOR

Eligio Stephen Gallegos, PhD,
PO Box 468
Velarde NM 87572
www.esgallegos.com

CONTACT MOON BEAR PRESS

www.MoonBearPress.com
orders@moonbearpress.com

BOOKS BY E.S. GALLEGOS, PH.D.

The Personal Totem Pole Process: Animal Imagery, The Chakras and Psychotherapy ISBN 0-944164-09-9
Kindle version also available: ISBN 0-944164-10-2
Animals of the Four Windows: Integrating Thinking, Sensing, Feeling and Imagery, ISBN 0-944164-40-4.
Little Ed & Golden Bear, ISBN 0-944164-12-9.

STORIES FOR THE INNER CHILD SERIES:

Nothing is Nothing, Book 1 ISBN-10 0-944164-24-2 by Steve Gallegos (E.S. Gallegos Ph.D.), 2013
Something is Something, Book 2 ISBN-13: 978-0-944164-28-0 by Steve Gallegos (E.S. Gallegos Ph.D.), 2014
Dream Visits, Book 3, ISBN-13: 978-0-944164-30-3 by Steve Gallegos (E.S. Gallegos Ph.D.), 2015

COMING SOON:

Stories for the Inner Child Collection: Eagle Wisdom, Books 1-9, by Steve Gallegos (E.S. Gallegos Ph.D.), 2018
Control and Obedience: The Human Illness by E.S. Gallegos Ph.D. 2018

OTHER BOOKS ON IMAGERY FROM MOON BEAR PRESS

The Circus Cage: A Journey of Transformation
by Rosalie G. Douglas. ISBN 978-0944164020

Dancing in my Grandfather's Garden: Unearthing the Soul of the Feminine and the Gift of Deep Imagery,
by Phyllis Brooks Licis. ISBN: 978-0944164181

ABOUT THE AUTHOR

Eligio Stephen Gallegos (aka Steve) was born the state of New Mexico in the southwestern United States in 1934. Of Native American, English and Irish descent, Steve was raised in the local Hispanic culture speaking both English and Spanish. A gifted craftsman he was involved in woodcarving, leatherwork, silverwork, and drawing and painting from an early age and greatly disliked the confinement and regimentation of school even though he was an intellectually gifted student.

After military service, he completed his undergraduate work at the University of Wisconsin, his masters at New Mexico State and his Ph.D. in Psychology at Florida State University. He taught at Mercer University, Macon, Georgia between 1967-1981. After fourteen years as professor of psychology in Macon, GA, Steve undertook a residency in psychotherapy in the State of Oregon and became a practicing psychotherapist.

While in Oregon, Steve underwent a spiritual experience that changed him profoundly. This experience is described in the Personal Totem Pole Process (ISBN 9780944164099). He describes the experience as "spontaneously meeting the alivenesses that were rooted in my energy centers and that presented themselves primarily as animals, but they had to be approached through the knowing of the deep imagination. I realized that the teacher I had sought for my entire life was in fact deep within my imagination and had always been there."

Since then, introducing people to their own inner animals and the rediscovery of the wisdom of the imagination, has been his path in life. For over 30 years, he has taught people how to access their wholeness through developing a relationship with their deep imagination. Steve discovered and developed the Personal Totem Pole Process© as a way of meeting the inner animals and beings of the deep imagination.

Through his books and other writings, he has explored many healing aspects of the deep imagination. He holds that one of our major challenges is to return to balance between the ways of knowing, so that inking, Sensing, Feeling and Imagery are once again fully available to each of us, both for our own growing and the world's wholeness.

At present he is primarily engaged in offering workshops and in training others in the exploration of the deep imagination in the

United States, Ireland, Germany, Austria, France, Denmark, the
Czech Republic, Macedonia, Portugal, and Australia.

For further information on trainings, workshops and individual
sessions using the Personal Totempole Process© and Deep Imagery, please visit

www.esgallegos.com or

www.deepimagery.net

CREDITS

Cover: Design & preparation by Mary Diggin, Ph.D.
Editor: Mary Diggin, Ph.D. www.MaryDiggin.com
Photo of author: Raffaella Mayana Romieri

Original Book Layout © 2017 BookDesignTemplates.com

Template edited and reformatted by Mary Diggin

CPSIA information can be obtained
at www.ICGtesting.com
Printed in the USA
LVHW080231290421
685944LV00010B/288

9 780944 164495